Symbolic and
Pragmatic Semantics

Susan S. Bean

Symbolic and Pragmatic Semantics

A Kannada System of Address

The University of Chicago Press
Chicago and London

SUSAN S. BEAN lived for a year in a village near Bangalore, India, and is currently assistant professor of anthropology at Yale University.

The University of Chicago Press, Chicago 60637
The University of Chicago Press, Ltd., London

©1978 by The University of Chicago
All rights reserved. Published 1978
Printed in the United States of America

82 81 80 79 78   5 4 3 2 1

Library of Congress Cataloging in Publication Data

Bean, Susan S
Symbolic and pragmatic semantics.

Bibliography: p.
Includes index.
1. Kannada language—Address, Forms of.
2. Kannada language—Semantics.   3. Kannada
language—Social aspects.   4. Pragmatics.
I. Title.
PL4649.B4   494'.814'2   77-18198
ISBN 0-226-03989-7

to my mother
Edith Sycle Sharf
(1915–1976)
for her gift of strength

Contents

Acknowledgments

I wish to thank my colleagues Vishwanath Ayengar, H. Blustain, N. Bonvillian, H. C. Conklin, W. Mc-Cormack, H. Pitkin, H. W. Scheffler, C. M. Scotton, and S. Tyler for their insightful and constructive comments on various drafts of this manuscript.

For the research on which this study is based I gratefully acknowledge the support of the National Institutes of Mental Health.

Most of all, I am indebted to the people of Avaruuru for their hospitality and cooperation.

Introduction

The speakers of any language have at their disposal a
number of expressions for addressing one another.
In most languages the vocabulary of terms for address is highly elaborated, and use of the expressions
is governed by complex rules of etiquette. The study
of terms for address should therefore be of special
interest to linguists and anthropologists in general,
especially those interested in the relationship between language structure and the social structures of
speech communities. It is, however, a relatively un-
explored subject. The linguistic and anthropological
literature contains many studies of one or another
subset of the total vocabulary of terms for address.
However, to my knowledge no one has as yet produced a study of the semantic structure of the total
vocabulary of terms for address in any one language
(those who come the closest are Chao 1956 and
Cooke 1968). It seems probable that one of the reasons, if not the major reason, for the relatively un-
derdeveloped state of the study of terms for address
is that until recently the theoretical concepts essential to such studies have not been available. This
study of terms for address in Kannada, one of the
four main Dravidian languages of South India, is
intended as a remedy (even if only partial) for both
these deficiencies.

By and large, the study of lexical meaning has
been conceived as the study of words that are about

things, actions, relationships, that is, concepts in a cultural system. Unlike most other vocabularies, terms of address are not simply *about* something, that is, used to discuss categories of the sociocultural world; they are tied to their referents indexically, necessarily being copresent with them. A term of address does not simply say who is the addressee of a particular utterance, it makes him the addressee by being directed at him. That terms of address have been the subject of sociolinguistic analysis as often as of semantic analysis, suggests an implicit recognition of their double mode of signification, symbolic (traditional semantic) and pragmatic (indexical). An appreciation of this special dual status illuminates other, related problems. For example, one can account for the traditional exclusion of terms of address in the analysis of kin classification systems: vocative forms are kinship terms that refer to kin categories, and, simultaneously, they are part of the speech act in which they occur and therefore must be related to it, as well as to the abstract conceptual system of kin classification. It is because of their dual status that they are often not good reflectors of kin categories.[1]

Terms of address, because they are tied to the social organization of the speech act, are one of those phenomena that make it impossible to treat language as a wholly autonomous system. Similar linguistic phenomena are other shifters or deictics, forms which orient the utterances in which they occur to the social, spatial, and temporal dimensions of the speech act (e.g., tense markers, demonstratives of time and place). There is now a trend away from the analysis of language as an autonomous system, an approach which typified linguistics during most of this century. Linguistic sign systems were characteristically studied independently of meaning (e.g., Bloomfieldian linguistics, Chomsky 1957, 1965), and independently of their relations to the situations in which they are used (all linguistics, except perhaps the British influenced by Malinowski). Representative of the current attention to the pragmatic and semantic bases of linguistic sign systems are the interests in deixis (Jakobson 1957, Fillmore 1971a, Silverstein 1976); the theory of speech acts, in which the use of language is viewed as the performance of various acts like promising, questioning, declaring (e.g., Ross 1970, Sadock 1974, Searle 1969); and in the theory of presuppositions, which ties grammatical analysis to the knowledge of the participants in the speech act (e.g., Lakoff 1971, Fillmore 1971b).

For linguistic anthropology the enthusiastic adoption of Morris's paradigm distinguishing syntactics, semantics, and pragmatics is an important landmark in the decline of autonomous linguistics. The relationship of signs in a system (syntactics) was, for Morris, the subject of grammar and, it was supposed, could be analyzed separately from the uses and meanings of signs (Morris 1946). This formulation appealed to anthropologists who were beginning to work in semantics (e.g., Goodenough 1956, Lounsbury 1956) and pragmatics (e.g., Hymes 1962). But the growth of interest in semantics and pragmatics has led to challenges of the autonomy of sign systems. In generative semantics and speech act theory the barriers collapse between syntax, semantics, and pragmatics: the basis of grammatical structure is semantic, and the organization and meaning of signs is a function of the acts they are used to perform.

Terms of address stand in the interstice between semantics and pragmatics, since their meaning is in part *about* the sociocultural world and in part *in their connection* to the social situation in which they occur. Because their meaning is in part "about" (i.e., symbolic) and in part "by connection" (i.e., indexical or pragmatic), their analysis presents a challenge for lexical semantics, traditionally the study only of symbolic meaning. In order to incorporate the analysis of pragmatic meaning into lexical semantics, I suggest additions to theory and method. Address cannot be treated as a semantic domain unless this is done: the names, pronouns, kinship terms, and status terms that compose the address terminology have no symbolic semantic features in common. Address emerges as a semantic domain only by recognizing its unity in the pragmatic meaning of address terms, "directed at the addressee."

The first chapter provides this extension of ethnographic semantics, making it possible to proceed with the formal semantic analysis of the address terminology, the subject of the rest of the study. The corpus of address terms falls into three major subsets: second person markers, kinship terms, and personal names. Each of these subsets shares few semantic features with any of the others, so that definitions emerge primarily from the contrasts among the members of a subset. For that reason the terms in each subset are first analyzed independently, as part of the pronominal system, the kin classification system, and the system of personal names. The last chapter brings together the results of the analyses of the subsets of address terms and presents the semantic structure of the address terminology in its entirety. An important product of this semantic analysis is the distinction between definitions, sociolinguistic variables that influence the selection of terms with particular definitions, and the communicative functions of terms of address in speech acts.

Because terms of address are indexical symbols having both pragmatic and symbolic meaning, they are twice social: they refer to social identities, and they are, by definition, tied to the dyadic, face to face interactions in which they occur. In contemporary anthropology and sociology the nature of face to face encounters and microsociology (e.g., the work of Goffman, ethnomethodology, the transactional analysis of Barth and Bailey) are subjects of considerable attention. The distinctive character of dyadic sociations is generally recognized, but the relationship between encounters and the organization of the larger society (macrosociology) remains to be understood. Terms of address are especially relevant to this issue because they are mediators between the structure of encounters and the organization of society as a whole. The social organization of all speech acts is basically similar: the nature of the speech signal constructs a social relationship that is dyadic and face to face. Yet, because relatively few people in any community are prohibited from participating in such interactions with each other, participants in a speech act may bring almost any combination of social identities to it. It is the job of terms of address to mediate between universal properties of sociation in speech acts and the diversity of social statuses represented by speaker and addressee.

The Kannada address system achieves this by being based on features that are primitives of all social orders: the principles of age, sex, and genealogical connection, on which recruitment to other social statuses is based; and relationships in social space (social distance, role distance, and hierarchy). Address terms mediate the dyadic sociation of the speech act and the structure of the society by expressing the social distance and hierarchy (sometimes a matter of age, sex, and genealogical connection) appropriate to the relative statuses of addressee and speaker.

I chose to do this study in India because I expected to find a complex system of address reflecting the highly stratified character of Indian caste society. That I did not find such a system, that the address system described here is relatively simple, has turned out to be a stimulus rather than a disappointment. I began with a question about the relationship between semantic structures and social structures; I found out that this was a good question to ask since the level of correspondence between linguistically labeled categories and social categories cannot be assumed, but must be discovered in the process of analysis.

I chose India for this study also because the social organization of rural communities in South Asia is well known. Since the linguistic portion of the research depended upon knowing who, socially, a speaker is and what his relationship is to the other addressed or referred to, working in a well-studied area simplified the ethnographic portion of the research: I knew what to expect and, therefore, the relevant questions to ask.

The research for this study was done near the city of Bangalore in Avaruuru, a small agricultural village with 120 households of middle and low ranking castes (there were no Brahmins). There are four sub-castes (*jaati*) of Hindus (74 households). The Kuruba jaati (20 households) is economically and politically dominant in the village; its members own most of the land. The Vokkaliga jaati (6 households), of equal or somewhat higher rank than the Kurubas, recently settled in the village with the cooperation of some Kuruba families. The people of the BeeDa jaati (5 households), considerably lower ranking, are all descended from a Vokkaliga man and a BeeDa woman who ran off together and came to live in the village a generation ago. The A.K. jaati, *aadi karnaataka*[2] ("original inhabitants of Karnataka") (40 households), is an untouchable caste economically tied to the Kurubas, whose lands they cultivate. Another 45 households are Roman Catholics of two jaatis whose ancestors converted and migrated from Tamil and Telugu speaking areas. Tamil or Telugu is still their first language. (The one remaining house consists of a Muslim woman and her two children.)

Linguistic data were collected in two ways: by intensive tape-recorded interview, usually with one person (my recording equipment would allow no more sophisticated arrangement); and by listening and recording the words people used to talk to and about others. A distinction was maintained between what people say they ought to say, what people say they say, and what people actually say. Since there is considerable overlap between these classes of data, I have chosen not to present them separately, but to discuss the differences whenever they appear to be relevant. In some chapters estimates are made of the frequency of use of forms, for example, "often," "seldom," "never," in order to distinguish the usual from the unusual or nonoccurring. No attempt was made to quantify the data: quantification is not an appropriate technique for the elucidation of semantic structures where rare usages may be as illuminating as common ones.

Below is the phonemic inventory of the Kannada spoken in the village:[3]

Consonants

	Labial	Dental	Retroflex	Palatal	Velar	Glottal
Stops (all unaspirated)						
voiceless	p	t	T	c	k	
voiced	b	d	D	j	g	
Continuants						
nasal	m	n	N		ŋ	
oral voiceless		s		š		h
oral voiced	v	l	L	y		
		r				

Vowels

	Front (Unrounded)	Back (Rounded)
High	i	u
Mid	e	o
Low		a	

LENGTH: Length is phonemic for vowels and consonants. In this transcription, long vowels and consonants will be written as double: e.g., /d/ a short consonant and /dd/ a long consonant.

1 | Pragmatic Meaning and Address

Indexicality and Pragmatic Meaning

Terms of address are indexical symbols, and their analysis requires an appreciation of the distinction between symbolic and pragmatic meaning·and techniques for analyzing both. The concepts of symbolic and pragmatic meaning used in this study are derived from the classification of signs developed by the philosopher Charles Peirce. In Peirce's work the "fundamental division of signs" is a trichotomous distinction between icon, index, and symbol based on the relationships between signs and their objects.[1] The icon represents its object by possessing some attribute similar to it. The index indicates its object by being existentially associated with it. The symbol refers to its object through an arbitrary association established by convention (Peirce 1932, Buchler 1940, Burks 1949). While the iconic, indexical, and symbolic are distinguishable as three modes of signification, many, if not most, signs participate simultaneously in more than one of these modes of signification.[2]

Languages are sign systems predominantly utilizing the symbolic mode of signification. Segments of sound come to be signs of objects and concepts through an arbitrary association established by conventional usage. For example, *bekku* in Kannada, *chat* in French, *cat* in English are signs arbitrarily related to their objects, and it is only by convention among the members of each speech community that they designate similar classes of animals. The arbitrary relationship between signs and what they stand for is often presented as the hallmark of language, that which distinguishes human language from the sign systems of all other creatures. Students of language recognize, however, that the symbolic mode is not the only mode of signification that occurs in languages.

Signs with a significant iconic component occur in all languages. Onomatopoeic expressions are supposed to represent what they stand for by a likeness of sound (e.g., *moo* for the sound produced by cows, *crackle* for the sound of a fire). The phenomenon usually referred to as "sound symbolism" is, in terms of the modes of signification defined above, also iconic. The configuration of the vocal tract during the articulation of a sign represents, by similarity, what it stands for. For example, in many languages words for near or small contain close vowels such as *i,* and words for distant or large contain open vowels such as *a.* The close articulation is interpreted as an icon of 'small' or 'proximate', while the open articulation is interpreted as an icon of 'large' or 'distant' (for example, *this* and *that* in English, ii*ga* 'now' and aa*ga* 'then' in Kannada).

Linguistic signs with a significant indexical component are abundant in all languages, and one class of them, *shifters* or *deictics,* is indispensable to the functioning of a language because its members serve to orient the content of messages to the situations in which they are uttered. Thus linguistic messages, produced by a speaker in a particular spatial, temporal, and social setting, contain signs which denote properties of that situation, relating it to the content of the message. For example, in *The car is here, here* signifies the place at which *here* (and the utterance of which it is a part) was spoken; in *He came yesterday, yesterday* signifies the day before *yesterday* (and the utterance of which it is a part) was spoken. Another class of linguistic signs with a significant indexical component is proper names. These, I will argue in chapter 6, are indexical signs because an intrinsic association exists between the name and its bearer. Names are widely considered to belong to their bearers, and to be actually connected to or part of the self. In both English and Kannada *name* (Kannada *hesaru*) is used to mean reputation (e.g., *He is a big name in that field, avarige vaLLe hesar ide* 'he has a good name, i.e., reputation').

All signs 'stand for' (refer to) some cultural category (object); it is by doing so that signs can be said to mean (signify, connote).[3] A sign functioning symbolically, that is, arbitrarily related to its object, signifies the distinctive attributes of the class it designates. For example, for something to be said to be *near* something else, the two things must be in a close spatial relationship. Thus the word *near* may be said to signify a 'close spatial relationship'. Similarly, in order for an animal to be called a *kitten,* it must be an immature feline. Thus, *kitten* may be said to signify the properties 'feline-immature'.

A sign functioning indexically, in existential relationship with its object, presents a very different case. Such a sign signifies the intrinsic connection between it and its object. For example, for *clouds* to be understood as an indexical sign of rain, the clouds must be perceived in spatiotemporal relationship with the rain. Thus *clouds* may be said to signify the spatiotemporal relationship with rain. Similarly, to say of something that it is *here,* it must be in 'close spatial relationship to the place where *here* is uttered'. *Here* is an indexical symbol: it signifies symbolically 'close spatial relationship' (like *near*) and it signifies indexically 'relationship to the place of utterance' (unlike *near*).

These two kinds of relations between signs and designated cultural categories, symbolic and indexical, create two distinct kinds of meaning (signification). Symbolic meaning is a product of signs that are arbitrarily related to their objects and that therefore signify distinctive properties of the object class. Pragmatic (or indexical) meaning is a product of signs existentially associated with their objects, which therefore signify an intrinsic connection to their objects (but nothing further about the properties of the objects themselves).

Pragmatics and Pragmatic Meaning

The use of *pragmatic* in 'pragmatic meaning' presented in the preceding section is derived from Peirce and should be distinguished from another use of the term current in linguistic anthropology, that derived from the semiotic of Charles Morris. Morris's science of signs is divided into three topics: semantics, the study of the signification of signs; syntactics, the relations of signs to each other; and pragmatics (now usually called sociolinguistics), the relations between signs and their users (Morris 1946). Pragmatic meaning, characterized in the preceding section, belongs both within Morris's semantics, because it has to do with the signification of signs, and within his pragmatics, because it has to do with the relationship of signs to their uses and users. Morris did not distinguish the variety of signification I have called pragmatic meaning.

In Morris's scheme, two modes of signification are indispensable to statements: *identifiors,* which "signify the location of something or other, but do not signify anything else about this something or other" (Morris 1946, p. 76) and *designators,* which signify the properties of objects. Linguistic indexes, such as shifters, are included among the identifiors. By classifying them in this way, a crucial distinction among identifiors is ignored: some identifiors are fundamentally indexical and some are wholly symbolic. In the sentences *It happened yesterday* and *It happened Wednesday, yesterday* and *Wednesday* are both identifiors: they denote the day on which 'it happened'. But *yesterday* is a shifter meaning 'the day before the uttering of *yesterday*', and its meaning is therefore dependent on the situation of its utterance, specifically, the time of its utterance. In contrast, the meaning of *Wednesday* is unrelated to the time of its utterance and refers to 'the fourth day of the week', regardless of when *Wednesday* is uttered. The relationship between sign and object is fundamentally different. The meaning of *yesterday* is in part pragmatic, the relationship to the actual situation in which it is used, and in part symbolic, 'the day before'. In the case of an indexical sign, specification of its meaning (Morris's semantics) includes specification of a relationship of the sign to its situation of use (Morris's pragmatics). Linguistic indexes, because they have pragmatic meaning, constitute an intersection of Morris's semantics and pragmatics where signification is an aspect of use, thus dissolving a sharp distinction between semantics and sociolinguistics (Morris's pragmatics).

These observations make it possible to view some of the topics of linguistics from a fresh perspective. All speech is potentially an indexical sign of the speaker, the addressee, the time or place of speaking. What we call social dialect, for example, is an indexical sign of a social identity of the speaker (from hearing speech on the radio we can often tell if the speaker is Black, a Boston Brahmin, or, in Kannada, a Hindu Brahmin). In such cases, the listener understands not only the content of the encoded message, but also that the utterance has been produced by a speaker with a particular social identity.

Morris's model has been an important influence on linguistic anthropology, having the appeal of including not only the systems of signs (the traditional preserve of linguistics) but also their signification (semantics) and their use (pragmatics, sociolinguistics, the ethnography of communication). His greatest influence has been on ethnographic semantics, particularly on the development of the componential analysis of meaning. However, ethnographic semantics has been restricted largely to the study of Morris's *designators,* those signs which signify the properties of their objects, because the principal goal of the anthropological study of meaning in language has been to gain access to the knowledge and its organization that is encoded in language (e.g., genealogical and botanical classifications). Consequently, for ethnographic semanticists, meaning is conceived of as the attributes of classes of things to which linguistic labels refer. This kind of signification is, as was pointed out, a property of symbolic signs. In contrast, indexical signs, which signify an existential association with their objects, have pragmatic meaning, related to the uses and users of signs. Because the meaning of indexical signs is an aspect of the social and cultural situation of their use, they are of obvious significance for linguistic anthropology.

Indexical Features and Symbolic Features

Ethnographic semantics can be expanded to include pragmatic meaning as well as symbolic meaning. A basic tenet of ethnographic semantics is that the definitions of lexemes can be given in terms of the distinctive features of the categories they designate. The concepts and methods basic to this kind of semantic analysis were introduced to anthropology in two, now classic, papers by Goodenough and Lounsbury in 1956. Since then the concepts and methods that have become known as componential analysis have been used extensively in the analysis of kinship terminologies as well as in other vocabularies, such as those relating to plants and colors. This work of ethnographic semanticists has established componential analysis in anthropology as a basic method for the analysis of culturally significant vocabularies and, more widely, as a basic tool of semantic analysis.

Componential analysis may be characterized as a procedure for arriving at definitions of words in terms of semantic features or components. This kind of semantic analysis is usually performed on a set of linguistic terms whose meanings, while similar, contrast with each other on a limited set of dimensions. The similarity of meaning is represented as the root feature(s) of the semantic domain to which the terms belong. The denotata of each term are listed, and those attributes of the denotata that are always associated with a term, and which are different from those associated with other terms in the set, are the distinctive attributes. The distinctive attributes of each category and the root feature(s) constitute the definitions or significata of the terms in the set (for fuller explications see Goodenough 1967, Lounsbury 1964, Scheffler and Lounsbury 1971).

So far, discussions and applications of componential analysis have dealt only with symbolic meaning. Thus, semantic components or features whose combinations constitute the significata (definitions) of terms are described as attributes of the denotata (Goodenough 1967, p. 1203, Lounsbury 1964, p. 127, Scheffler and Lounsbury 1971, p. 3). This concentration on semantic features that are attributes of classes of denotata is the logical outcome of an interest in vocabularies of cultural things and concepts. In terms of the dichotomy being developed here, these are words whose definitions fall wholly within the symbolic mode of signification and therefore whose defining features are entirely symbolic. But as noted in the preceding sections, the symbolic mode of signification, in which sign and object are arbitrarily related, is but one of three ways in which signs may be related to their objects. In the indexical mode of signification, a sign does not signify attributes of its denotata (as does a symbolic sign), but rather signifies the existential association of the sign to its object. In order to incorporate the analysis of pragmatic meaning into ethnographic semantics, indexical features as well as symbolic features will be admitted as components of the significata of lexemes. By doing this it becomes possible to analyze Kannada address terminology, a system of indexical symbols incorporating elements of both pragmatic and symbolic meaning.

Pragmatic Meaning and the Theory of Language

Pragmatic meaning, as I have characterized it here, is of interest not only to anthropologists, because of its connection to cultural patterns and social life, but to linguists as well, because of its relations to grammatical theory. There is a growing interest, among students of language, in the pragmatic meanings of linguistic signs, although the term *pragmatic meaning* is not used by most of those studying it. One source of this interest is the work of the philosopher J. L. Austin. Austin distinguished three aspects of the speech act: the locutionary act, in which something is communicated; the illocutionary act, which reveals the speaker's intention in communicating something; and the perlocutionary act, which is the effect on the addressee of communicating something (Austin 1962). Austin's locutionary act communicates information about something and therefore consists primarily of what we have called symbolic meaning. By contrast, Austin's illocutionary act, which communicates the speaker's intention, does so by means of indexical signs that indicate what the speaker is doing in the act of utterance ('I promise that . . .', 'I declare that . . .'). The performative verbs *I declare, I promise* have pragmatic (or indexical) elements of meaning, because saying *I promise,* that is, producing the sign, is actually doing something, that is, 'promising'. Thus the sign *I declare* is existentially associated with its object, 'the act of declaring' (or, one could say, uttering it *is* the act of declaring). An illocutionary act, therefore, rests in part on the pragmatic meanings of linguistic signs. Austin's discussion of speech acts, particularly his notion of illocutionary acts and illocutionary force, has been influential not only on the philosophy of language (e.g., Searle 1969), but on linguistics and anthropology (e.g., M. Foster 1974, Sadock 1974, Tambiah 1973) as well.

The influence of Austin's ideas on current linguistic theory is an expression of the increasing attention paid by linguists to nonlinguistic correlates of speaking. Generative semanticists propose that the most abstract representation of an utterance is a semantic one which is transformed into a surface form and actualized phonologically in a long series of steps. Some generative semanticists have come close to distinguishing between symbolic and pragmatic meaning by noting that the meanings of utterances are tied to the situations of utterance and that knowledge of the sociocultural setting is necessary for understanding the utterance (e.g., Lakoff 1970). A few, following Austin, have suggested that part of the abstract representation of every utterance is a performative verb that explicitly indicates what the speaker is doing by saying something. And it has been argued that an abstract performative is required for the interpretation of many kinds of sentences and may be postulated as part of every abstract semantic representation (Ross 1970; Sadock 1974). Some linguists have noticed that the orientational features of language, traditionally called *deictics,* similarly require knowledge of the social and spatiotemporal setting for their interpretation. They have shown how the correct interpretation of deictic categories requires taking into account the situation in which the utterance occurs, in terms of supposition rules (Fillmore 1966) or speakers' assumptions about the relationships between the speech event and the narrated event (Lakoff 1970).

None of these, however, explicitly confronts a distinction between modes of signification, and in fact most appear to assume that the only mode of signification is roughly what here is termed 'symbolic'. More radical proposals for the place of pragmatic meaning in the theory of language have been offered by Halliday (1970) and Silverstein (1976), who argue for a pragmatic grammar of language in contrast to a semantically (symbolically) based grammar to which pragmatic categories are added when necessary (as in the work of Ross, Sadock, Lakoff, and Fillmore mentioned above).

The recent attention to pragmatic meaning in linguistics is evidence that the peculiar qualities of indexical signs (whether or not explicitly so labeled) are being noticed by linguists; important implications for a theory of language are being recognized; and proposals for the place of indexicality in a theory of language are being considered. An interest in pragmatic meaning, then, is evidently growing in the philosophy of language, in linguistics, and in anthropology. It is in the context of these efforts that this analysis of address in Kannada should be considered.

Deictics as Indexical Symbols

Language is a social phenomenon. Spoken language, speech, does not exist apart from its use by particular people in a particular place at a particular time. That is, speech is situated socially, temporally, and spatially. All languages contain forms that express the relationship between the utterances produced and the social, temporal, and physical setting of the speech act. Traditionally these orientational elements of language are known as *deictics* and include pronouns, tense markers, demonstratives of time and place, as well as terms of address.

> Deixis is the name given to those aspects of a language whose interpretation is relative to the occasion of utterance; to the time of utterance, and to times before and after the time of utterance; to the location of the speaker at the time of utterance; and to the identity of the speaker and the intended audience. An extended theory of deixis would take in several other aspects of the speaker's spatial, temporal, and social orientation. [Fillmore 1966, p. 220]

The interpretation of deictic elements is always with reference to the source of the utterance, the speaker. When the role of speaker is transferred from one actor to another, the center of the deictic system shifts from the first speaker to the second. Because deictics are orientational features whose center changes with the source of the utterance, they have also been called *shifters,* a term coined by Jespersen (1922) and adopted by Jakobson (1957).

Because deictics or shifters signify an aspect of the spatial, temporal, and social setting in which they occur, and therefore relate the message to its situation of utterance, they are, in part, indexical signs with pragmatic meaning. Thus *I* indicates the person uttering *I* (Burks 1949, p. 678); *here* indicates a location near the person uttering *here;* and *now* indicates a time close to the time *now* is spoken. The existential association between the shifter and the social, spatial, or temporal situation of its utterance is the indexical component of its meaning. However, shifters like *here* and *now* are symbolic signs too that signify 'a place near the speaker' and 'a time near the time of speaking'. Notice that a fundamental element of meaning is lost in purely symbolic glosses: *here* means 'nearby' but only 'near' the speaker of *here,* not 'near' anything else.

Following Jakobson (1957, p. 3) we may characterize some of the classes of shifters commonly found in languages by means of four elements: the speech itself (^{s}), the narrated matter (^{n}), the event itself (E), and the participants in the event (P). "Consequently four items are to be distinguished: a narrated event (E^n), a speech event (E^s), a participant of the narrated event (P^n), and a participant of the speech event (P^s), whether addresser or addressee" (Jakobson 1957, p. 3). Shifters are classes that include reference to the speech itself (^{s}), that is, to the speech event or participants in the speech event. Using this scheme Jakobson discusses four classes of shifters:

1. $E^n E^s$ These are the forms that relate the narrated event to the speech event, such as tense markers and adverbs of time. In Kannada, for example, *avanu tooTakka hooda* 'he to-garden go-past-he', 'he went to the garden', the past tense marker on the verb, *-d-*, indicates that the narrated event (E^n, his going to the garden) occurred before the time of the speech event (E^s).

2. $P^n E^n/P^s$ "These are forms that characterize the relation between the narrated event (E^n) and its participants (P^n) with reference to the participants of the speech event (P^s)" (Jakobson 1957, p. 4) and include the mood of the verb, and other indicators of the illocutionary force of the speech act. For example, a question indicates the speaker's (P^s) inquiry about the persons and events referred to ($P^n E^n$): *avanu yelli hooda* 'where did he go?' Adverbials and adjectives of place also belong

to this class of shifters, because they relate the location of the persons and events narrated to the location of the participants in the speech event. For example, in *avanu alli hooda* 'he went there', *alli* 'there' is a shifter indicating that the participant in the narrated event ($P^n E^n$) is located at some distance from the speaker (P^s).

3. $E^n E^{ns}/E^s$ This class of shifters is labeled *evidential* by Jakobson "for the verbal category which takes into account three events—the narrated event, the speech event, and the narrated speech event (E^{ns}) namely the alleged sources of information about the narrated event. The speaker reports an event on the basis of someone else's report . . . dream . . ." (Jakobson 1957, p. 4). For example, in the sentence *avanu hooda andLu* 'he went, she said', the speech event is a report of an event ('he went', E^n) given on the evidence of a report made in another speech event ('she said' E^{ns}).

4. P^n/P^s This class of shifters, the one we shall be concentrating on, is traditionally called *person:* it "characterizes the participants of the narrated event with reference to the participants of the speech event" (Jakobson 1957, p. 4)—for example, *naanu hoode* 'I (speaker) went', *niinu hoogtiiya* 'will you-sg-(addressee) go?'

Jakobson's classification distinguishes shifters from nonshifters in that the former by definition include reference to the speech event or participants in the speech event. His classification of shifters is based on the relationships between aspects of that which is narrated (E^n, P^n) and aspects of speaking (E^s, P^s). Shifters may also be classified according to which orientational features of speaking they indicate. This is a more appropriate formulation for the purposes of this study, since the signification of an indexical sign is its existential relation to its object, here the social, temporal, and spatial dimensions of the speech act. Looked at in this way, there are four classes of shifters:

1. Shifters of person indicating the goal or source of utterance and distinguishing these from persons talked about (e.g., *I, you,* vs. *he*);
2. Shifters of function indicating the relationships of the speaker to the message, i.e., what the speaker is doing with the utterance (e.g., asking a question, christening a baby, making a statement, reporting a speech event);
3. Shifters of time relative to the moment of utterance (e.g., *now, then*);
4. Shifters of place relative to the location of the participants in the speech event (e.g., *here, there*).

The indexical semantic features of shifters would therefore be existential association with (a) the speaker or (b) the addressee, (c) the act performed by speaking, (d) the time of utterance, or the location of the (e) speaker or (f) addressee in the speech event.

As indexical symbols, shifters obliterate the usual distinction between semantics, the study of the meaning of linguistic signs, and sociolinguistics, the study of the uses of linguistic signs. The analysis of the indexical properties of shifters is simultaneously semantic and socioloinguistic, a study of signs whose definition is in part the situation of their use. Because shifters orient messages to the sociocultural situation of speaking, they are an important link between language and the sociocultural system.

The Speech Act

A communicative act requires (1) a sender who encodes and transmits a message, (2) the message itself, and (3) a receiver who decodes the message. The communicative acts we shall be concerned with are those which encode the message in speech. The speech signal consists of sound waves that are of short duration (Charles D. Hockett's "rapid fading" [1960]) which requires that the sender and receiver be relatively close to each other. Moreover, the subtlety of the acoustic features that distinguish meaning results in a low tolerance for simultaneous acoustic signals, both linguistic and nonlinguistic. Thus, while many speech signals can be sent simultaneously, only one can be effectively received at a time. Consequently, except under some special circumstances (e.g., choral singing) there can be only one speaker at a time.

The speech signal is public (Hockett's "broadcast transmission") and therefore can be received by anyone within earshot whether or not he/she is the designated recipient of the message.[4] This property of the speech signal is overlooked in much of the literature in which *hearer* and *addressee* are used synonymously. In fact, the two are distinct. The *addressee* is the intended recipient, and the *hearer* anyone who receives the message by virtue of being in earshot.

Thus while there can be only one speaker at a time, there may be several intended recipients or addressees. However, the paralinguistic visual communication that accompanies speaking (e.g., eye contact, head nodding, hand gestures) is difficult to maintain with more than one person at a time, and acoustic properties of the speech signal require special arrangements in order to transmit the signal to a group (e.g., sitting in a circle if several are to speak, placing all the addressees in front of the speaker if there is to be one principal speaker). Therefore, even if there are several addresses, all of them play the same role: since they receive the same signal from the same speaker, they are treated as one. Most speaking, then, occurs in dyadic interactions, and that which does not is facilitated by treating multiple addressees as one, as if the interaction were dyadic.

Just as it is necessary to distinguish between *addressee* and *hearer,* so we must distinguish between *speaker* and *addresser.* Speech signals can be produced that are not directed at anyone (e.g., when one says *damn* after stubbing a toe). It is possible to talk just to talk, but this is not the common use of speech. Therefore, although it is possible to distinguish an *addresser* as a speaker who directs the speech signal at a receiver in an attempt to communicate, the distinction is less often empirically significant than that between *addressee* and *hearer,* since most *speakers* are also *addressers,* while many *hearers* are not *addressees.*

These fundamental properties of speech and speaking determine some characteristics of the associated social interaction. There is only one speaker-addresser relatively close to one or more structurally equivalent hearer-addressee(s). The speech act therefore consists of three components: an addresser, an addressee, and an encoded message.[5] Although all three components are necessary for a communicative event to take place, the three components are not of equal status. There cannot be a receiver without a signal made available to him to decode, therefore the existence of a receiver is predicated on the existence of the signal. Further, the signal is dependent on the sender. Although the signal once emitted exists apart from the sender, it cannot come into existence without a sender. The existences of the message and the sender are, however, mutually dependent because an individual is a sender only while he produces a signal. That is, just as a signal cannot exist without a sender, a sender cannot exist without a signal. Since it is the sender who produces the signal, the signal is predicated on the sender, and the sender is therefore prior to the signal.

The relationship between the receiver and the signal is fundamentally different from the relationship between the sender and the signal. There is no mutual dependence. A speech signal cannot occur without a sender, but it can occur without a receiver. Thus the primitives of the speech act are the sender (or speaker) and the signal, not the receiver. It is the receiver, however, that transforms the speech act into a communicative act and the utterance into a message.[6] As will become clear in later chapters, recognition of these properties of the speech act is essential for the understanding of the semantic structure of the address system.

Terms for Address

Terms for address are shifters, that is, indexical symbols, whose meaning is in part symbolic and in part pragmatic (indexical). Since all terms for address are shifters which indicate the recipient of the message of which they are a part, address may be regarded as a pragmatic domain having an indexical root feature, 'existentially associated with the addressee'. The main portion of this monograph consists of the semantic analysis of Kannada terms for address as indexical symbols which have elements of pragmatic and symbolic meaning that can be specified in indexical and symbolic semantic features. The corpus of Kannada terms for address consists of second person forms, kinship terms, personal names, and a few nonkinship status terms.

Person forms constitute a pragmatic domain comprised of shifters (indexical symbols) which indicate roles in the speech act (speaker, addressee, and neither-speaker-nor-addressee). The pronominal system in Kannada distinguishes three persons and two numbers in independent pronouns and person affixes on verbs. The second person forms, in addition, may occur with markers signifying the sex and status of the addressee. The structure of the Kannada person system is the subject of chapter 2; the second person forms are the focus of chapter 3.

The kinship terms used in address belong to the Kannada system of kin classification, a symbolic domain whose root feature is 'relationship by blood or marriage'. The structure of this system is Dravidian, having, in addition to distinctions of sex and generation, a distinction between lineal and parallel collateral kintypes on the one hand and cross collateral kintypes on the other. The terms that label these kintypes are extended to more distant cross and parallel collateral kintypes by rules that typify Dravidian systems of kin classification. The terms for cross collateral kintypes are extended to relatives by marriage. Further, some kin terms are extended metaphorically to nonkin. Kinship terms designating senior kin classes occur frequently in address in both metaphoric and literal senses. The semantic structure of the system of kin classification is the subject of chapter 4, and kinship terms of address the subject of chapter 5.

Personal names constitute a pragmatic domain, but one whose indexical character is unlike that of shifters. Personal names are indexical in that they signify that their objects bear them (*George* signifies a man whose name is *George*); there is an intrinsic connection between the name and its bearer. Kannada personal names which occur frequently in address consist of god names or nicknames that often occur with kinship terms attached to them. The characteristics of Kannada personal names are discussed in chapter 6, and their occurrence in address analyzed in chapter 7. In the final chapter the several subdomains are articulated and the structure of the pragmatic domain of address is presented in its entirety.

The Semantic Structure of the Kannada Person System

Pronominal systems are excellent vehicles for demonstrating the advantages of a componential analysis of semantic structures. Indeed, personal pronouns were among the first lexical sets to be analyzed componentially (Austerlitz 1959, McKaughan 1959, Thomas 1955). Conklin's (1962) representation of the semantic structure of Hanunóo pronouns has a special place in this literature. His analysis improved on those of similar Philippine pronominal systems by Thomas and McKaughan, and provided a basis for subsequent analyses of the pronominal systems of unrelated languages (e.g., Berlin 1963, Buchler and Freeze 1966, Hymes 1972).

Traditionally the semantic structure of personal pronouns is represented in a diagram giving person (first, second, and third) vertically, and number (singular, dual, plural, etc.) horizontally. When Hanunóo pronouns are presented in this way the results appear awkward, because the dual class has only one member:

	Singular	Dual	Plural
1st person exclusive	*kuh*	—	*mih*
1st person inclusive	—	*tah*	*tam*
2d person	*muh*	—	*yuh*
3d person	*yah*	—	*dah*

The difficulty seems to be that the traditional category of number is inappropriate. Thomas,

McKaughan, and Conklin are satisfied with representing the category of person in terms of the presence or absence of the speaker (S) or hearer (H). However, their treatments of number are diverse, and Conklin's is clearly the most satisfactory. McKaughan is forced to argue that the form *tah* 'we two' is not plural because "both the speaker and the hearer are single individuals" (McKaughan 1959, p. 101). Thomas's analysis requires a division of the paradigm into "true pronouns" and "number pronouns," the former having the features "simple" or "plus," and the latter "singular" or "plural." This solution is less economical and, moreover, not semantically motivated. Conklin proposes, in addition to the oppositions 'speaker'/'not speaker' and 'hearer'/'not hearer', the opposition 'minimal membership'/'nonminimal membership'. Thus, any combination of ±S, ±H is considered minimal membership; that is, S̄H̄, S̄H, and also SH (traditionally dual). In this way the troublesome first person dual (*tah* in Hanunóo) is represented as MSH (i.e., minimal membership, including the speaker and hearer), and the first person plural inclusive is represented as M̄SH (i.e., including the speaker, the hearer, and some others). The result is a model in which the eight Hanunóo pronouns are distinguished by the combination of three binary oppositions (±S, ±H, ±M), a perfect paradigm in which the values of each dimension of contrast combine with each of the values of the other dimensions of contrast:

dah	M̄S̄H̄	'they'
yuh	M̄S̄H	'you all'
mih	M̄SH̄	'we'
tam	M̄SH	'we all'
yah	MS̄H̄	'he/she'
muh	MS̄H	'you'
kuh	MSH̄	'I'
tah	MSH	'we two'

The simplicity and symmetry of Conklin's model of the Hanunóo pronominal system is, unfortunately, not attainable for many other pronominal systems, because most of these (including English and Kannada) are not perfect paradigms and include features of limited distribution, such as gender, which often occurs only in third person forms. Happily, however, because the three semantic oppositions, ±speaker, ±hearer, ±minimal membership, are apparently universal features of

pronominal systems, Conklin's model has provided an excellent prototype for the analysis of the pronominal systems of other languages
(e.g., Buchler and Freeze 1966, Berlin 1963).

Conklin's model will be used as a prototype for the analysis of the
Kannada pronominal system, with three additions. First, the purpose of
the componential analyses of pronouns has been to demonstrate the
superiority of emic analyses over traditional analyses of lexical sets. In
the process, however, the model constructed displays, without acknowledging as such, the apparently universal features of pronominal systems. While pronominal systems differ from one another, and each must
be presented as a distinct semantic system, pronominal systems are in
significant respects similar, and semantic analyses should take into account these similarities as well. A consideration of the universal properties of pronominal systems will be presented below. Second, I will argue
that 'speaker' and 'addressee' are indeed universal features of pronominal systems, but are features of pragmatic meaning, not, as has been
assumed, features of symbolic meaning. Third, all paradigms, by definition, have a root meaning usually represented in a common feature
(Lounsbury 1964, Conklin 1962). However, the semantic unity of a
pronominal set has yet to be specified. I will attempt to do so here.

The Domain of Person and the
Indexical Features S and A

One of the purposes of componential analysis is to discover the semantic
structure of the pronominal system of a language and not merely to
describe it in terms of person and number in a manner developed for the
grammars of classical Indo-European languages. The latter sort of
analysis, it is argued, can obscure or distort the structures of languages
unlike Indo-European. By using the methods of componential analysis,
the semantic structure of a pronominal system can be elucidated from
the obligatory contrasts that distinguish the meanings of the pronominal
forms in that particular system. The componential analyses of pronominal systems cited earlier each attempt to do this. In attending to the
necessary task of accurately describing particular systems, however,
they have tended to overlook the profound similarities among pronominal systems that have their source in the nature of the speech act.

The speech act, as discussed in chapter 1, is essentially a dyadic sociation between a speaker who sends a message and the intended recipient, or addressee. Pronouns are definable in relation to the roles in the speech act distinguishing nonparticipants from participants, and, among the latter, addressee from speaker: 'first person' forms are those used by the speaker to indicate himself, 'second person' forms are those used by the speaker to indicate the addressee, and 'third person' forms are those used to refer to persons and things that are neither speaker nor addressee (i.e., not participants in the speech act). The third person is distinct from the first and second in that it is negatively defined as nonparticipant. Therefore, unlike the referents of first- and second-person forms, third-person referents need not be capable of participation in speech acts, and may or may not be present during the speech act. Because of this, there are often more semantic distinctions, such as sex, definiteness, and proximity, within the third-person category than within the first or second.

The prominence of the features 'speaker' and 'addressee' (or 'hearer') in semantic analyses of pronominal systems (except Austerlitz 1959) is a reflection of the relationship between pronominal systems and the social organization of speaking. But the features 'speaker' and 'addressee' have not been adequately understood. Like most semantic analyses, those of pronominal systems have been restricted to symbolic meaning. As pointed out in chapter 1, a purely symbolic definition of pronouns is inadequate because it does not take into account that the pronoun is intrinsically connected to the speech act: I denotes only the speaker who utters I. Similarly *you* denotes the recipient of *you,* and *he* denotes neither its speaker nor its recipient. Thus the features 'speaker' and 'addressee' are indexical significata representing the existential connection between sign and object: e.g., 'the speaker of I (or *naanu*)', 'the addressee of *you* (or *niinu*)'.

The indexical features 'speaker' S^1 and 'addressee' **A** are universals of the semantic structure of pronominal systems and reflect universal properties of the speech act. Like all members of the class of shifters discussed in chapter 1, they are defined by connection to the speech act. Person shifters apparently occur in all languages. All the semantic analyses of pronominal systems referred to earlier in this chapter assert that personal pronouns constitute a semantic paradigm, yet they consider only the semantic features that distinguish the meanings of the terms in the set from each other and not the root meaning that unites the members of the paradigmatic set. The property usually referred to as common to all pronouns is their function as personal name substitutes (Conklin 1962), a class of noun substitutes (Bloomfield 1933, Postal 1970), but this is a syntactic, not a semantic, property. (Moreover, although it is often accurate to characterize third-person pronouns as name substitutes that function anaphorically, this description is problematic in the case of first- and second-person pronouns.)

It is generally accepted that a semantic domain or field is a conceptual entity that is partitioned and labeled linguistically, and that the unity of the domain consists in a semantic feature or features that are shared by all the categories within it (Lounsbury 1964, Conklin 1962). This may be true for paradigms such as kinship, or taxonomic hierarchies such as plant classifications, but it need not be, and indeed is not, the only way that a semantic domain may be unified. There are at least two other possibilities. The definitions of the terms that partition the domain may be related to each other by rules that join one to another. For example, a disjunctive class does not have a comprehensive componential definition, but may be described by rules extending labels from one subclass of referents to another. The domain of *relatives* in American English has been described in this way (Scheffler 1976). Also, a domain may be delimited by an exhaustive intersection of variables. Thus the unity of the domain is expressed by the complete combination of two or more features, although classes within the domain have no single semantic feature in common. This is apparently the case in person systems. The domain of person shifters is delimited by the possible combinations of the indexical features of the two participants ('speaker' **S** and 'addressee' **A**) giving

$$S\overline{A}$$
$$SA$$
$$\overline{S}A$$
$$\overline{S}\,\overline{A}$$

There are three possible ways of representing the combinations of these features. In the first, the features are accorded equal importance in the speech act so that the four combinations, $S\overline{A}$, SA, $\overline{S}A$, $\overline{S}\,\overline{A}$, are logically and structurally equivalent. This is the position taken in most semantic analyses of pronominal systems (e.g., Conklin 1962, Berlin 1963). In the second and third, the features are ordered such that the addressee is prior (e.g., Hymes 1972), or the speaker is prior. I will argue that the third possibility is the correct one: the role of speaker is prior to that of addressee. In the first chapter it was shown that, although both speaker and addressee are necessary for a communicative act, the speaker is existentially prior to the addressee, since the production of a message is predicated on the existence of the speaker, while the presence of the addressee transforms the speech act into a communicative act. This is reflected in the person systems of languages. It may be significant that traditional accounts of person systems have been content to describe three persons and to include both $\overline{\text{SA}}$ forms and **SA** as first person (for an exception and for the proposal of a fourth person **SA**, see Hymes 1972). When the speaker indicates himself, the sender, he may include the addressee or others in his group. But when the speaker indicates the addressee, he is differentiating the receiver, the designated recipient of the message, and in so doing cannot logically include himself in the receiver's group, for that would negate the contrast between sender and receiver which it is the function of second person terms to express.

The appropriateness of this solution is demonstrated by the ease with which it permits the relationships between exclusive and inclusive first person plurals to be represented in Southern Dravidian languages. In Kannada, unlike proto-Dravidian and most other Southern Dravidian languages, there is no distinction between inclusive (**SAM**) and exclusive ($\overline{\text{SAM}}$) first person plural pronouns. The neutralization of the opposition between presence or absence of addressee in first person forms must be expressed in the way that most simply represents the loss of the distinction in Kannada. If 'speaker' is taken as prior, it is easy to do so; if 'addressee' is taken as prior, the result is very complex. In figure 2.1 the inclusive (**SA**) and the exclusive ($\overline{\text{SA}}$) are distinguished by a single

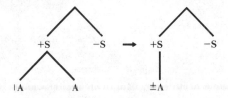

Figure 2.1

opposition which, if neutralized, dispenses with the contrast between inclusive and exclusive first person. In figure 2.2 no simple neutralization can suspend the contrast between inclusive and exclusive, since **AS** and **A̅S̅** are distinguished by three oppositions.

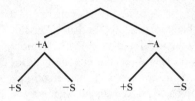

Figure 2.2

These considerations suggest that the basis of person systems may be represented in the key diagram given as figure 2.3.[2]

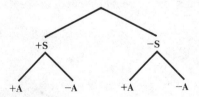

Figure 2.3

Number

Another apparent universal of pronominal systems is inclusion of number as a dimension of contrast (Forchheimer 1953, Ingram 1971a). Unlike person, number is not derived from the social organization of the speech act, and its universality may be related to the grammatical function of pronouns. Semantically, however, it is easy to see that nonsingular person pronouns are unlike many or most other plurals. Number in pronominal systems is not simply a distinction between one and many, but an expression of the complexity of nonsingular numbers in pronominal systems. Whereas *apples* means 'more than one apple', first person plural does not mean 'more than one speaker'. There can only be one speaker, and first person plural includes, in addition to the speaker, one or more addressees or others. Second person plural includes one or more addressees or others, but never the speaker. Third person plural includes more than one other, but never the speaker or the addressee. (We may note, then, that any pronominal form that includes the speaker (**S**) is first person; any that includes the addressee but not the speaker (**SA̅**) is second person; and any that excludes both (**S̅A̅**) is third person.)

As noted above, an opposition between minimal membership and nonminimal membership was proposed by Conklin (1962) to account for distinctions usually analyzed in terms of number, and his proposal has been adopted in most of the subsequent analyses cited above. This opposition operates on the output of the person key, so that **S̅A̅**, **S̅A**, **SA̅**, **SA** are each considered as a distinct category with minimal membership (although **SA** includes two actors). When recursively applied, this opposition distinguishes singular from plural, and dual and trial from plural as well.

For Kannada, which has only singular and plural numbers, and no opposition between inclusive and exclusive, the dimension of minimal membership operates simply on the output of the person key (fig. 2.4).[3]

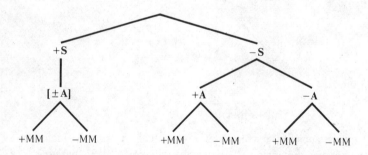

Figure 2.4

Apparently, then, there are two universal semantic dimensions in pronominal systems, one of pragmatic meaning, the other of symbolic meaning: person and number. These dimensions are ordered (±speaker, ±addressee, ±minimal membership) and provide a universal basic structure for the description of all pronominal systems, to which additional particular features of a pronominal system may be added, and its own unique structure elucidated. The Kannada pronomi-

nal system is analyzed on the basis of this proposed universal structure
of pronominal systems.

The Semantic Structure of Kannada Person Forms

The pronouns of Kannada are given in table 2.1 in traditional fashion,
according to person and number, with appropriate English glosses.
Fourteen pronouns are displayed in the person-number grid. Four
additional forms are given. Two of these latter are interrogative pronouns that together cover all fourteen of the forms given in the person-
number grid. The other two additional forms are marginal to the system:
they are structurally anomalous and occur rarely. These four forms will
be discussed separately. The fourteen forms constitute a paradigm: the
sense of each contrasts with the sense of every other on the basis of a
limited set of semantic features. In addition to contrasting on the dimensions of person and number, the fourteen pronouns contrast on the
dimensions of sex (the glosses 'he', 'she', 'it'), and distance (the
glosses 'close' and 'remote'). Further, three of the terms (*niivu, ivaru,
avaru*) have a second sense, polite address or reference to an individual.
Elsewhere I have accounted for these as metaphoric senses of the pronouns (Bean 1970, 1975a). I will review this argument below after
establishing the literal definitions of the terms.

In addition to the independent pronouns, there are person-number

Table 2.1   **Kannada Pronouns**

	Singular	Plural
1st Person	*naanu* 'I'	*naavu* 'we'
2d Person	*niinu* 'thou'	*niivu* 'you, ('thou, polite')
3d Person	*idu* 'it, close'	*ivu* 'these ones'
	adu 'it, remote'	*avu* 'those ones'
	ivaLu 'she, close'	*avaru* 'they, re-
	avaLu 'she, remote'	mote', ('he/she
	ivanu 'he, close'	remote polite')
	avanu 'he, remote'	*ivaru* 'they, close', ('he/she close polite')
Interrogative Pronoun:	*yaaru* 'who'	
	yaavadu 'which one'	
Marginal Forms:	*taavu* 'thou, honorific'	
	niivugaLu 'you, polite'	

suffixes that occur in some verb forms. The Kannada verb consists morphologically of a root inflected with two classes of suffixes: a tense-mode suffix (nonpast, past, contingent, perfect, negative), and a person-number suffix. There are three sets of person-number suffixes, each containing nine morphemes. One set occurs on nonpast stems (I), a second on past stems (II), and the third on contingent stems (III). Table 2.2 gives the pronouns with glosses followed by corresponding person-number suffixes.

Table 2.2	**Kannada Person-Number Suffixes**			
Pronoun	Gloss	Person-Number Suffix		
		I	II	III
naanu	'I'	*-iini*	*-e*	*-eenu*
naavu	'we'	*-iivi, -iiri*	*-vi*	*-vu*
niinu	'thou'	*-ii, -iiya*	*-ee*	*-ya, -ye*
niivu	'you'	*-iiri*	*-ri*	*-ra*
ivaLu	'she, close'	*-aaLe*	*-Lu*	*-Lu*
avaLu	'she, remote'			
ivanu	'he, close'	*-aane*	*-a*	*-nu*
avanu	'he, remote'			
ivaru	'they, close'	*-aare*	*-ru*	*-ru*
avaru	'they, remote'			
idu	'it, close'	*-ute*	*-tu*	*-tu*
adu	'it, remote'			
ivu	'these ones'	*-ve*	*-vu*	*-vu*
avu	'those ones'			

The correspondence of the pronouns to the person-number suffixes is effected by the neutralization of the opposition between close and remote distance which is distinctive for third-person pronouns, but not for third-person–number suffixes. All other contrasts that are distinctive for pronouns are distinctive for person-number suffixes. The opposition between remote and close distance is of the lowest order, since it is not distinctive in the person-number suffixes.

Kannada imperatives have a separate set of person-number suffixes that are added to the root uninflected for tense-mode:

Imperative Person-number suffixes	*Gloss*
-la	'let me _____?'
-ooNa	'let us _____'
(form identical with verb root)	'_____ thou'
-i, -ri	'_____ you'
-li	'let him/her/them/it _____'

For example, *hoogu* 'go' (root):

hoogla   'may I go'
hoogooNa   'let's go'
hoogu 'go thou'
hoogi, hoogri 'go you', 'go thou, polite'
hoogli 'let him, it, her, them go'

There are five imperative person-number suffixes corresponding to the fourteen personal pronouns. The reduction is effected by the neutralization of all oppositions distinguishing third-person pronouns (sex, distance, number).

In addition the 'thou' imperative may be modified by one of several vocative clitics:

-ee 'socially close female addressee' (*hoogee*)
-gee 'socially close female addressee' (used only to and by speakers of the A.K. jaati, *hoogegee*)'
-oo, -alee Socially close male addressee' (*hoogoo, hoogalee*).

Of the two interrogative pronouns, *yaaru* 'who' may be answered by any of the first- and second-person pronouns and the rational third-person pronouns (glossed 'he', 'she', 'they'); *yaavadu* 'which one' may be answered by any of the nonrational third-person pronouns (those glossed 'it' and 'ones'). This reflects the division of Kannada nouns into a rational and a nonrational class. The former consists of humans and gods, the latter of animals and inanimate things. A feature 'rational' is redundant in the first- and second-person pronouns since all speakers and addressees, by definition, fall into this class. The opposition is realized only in the third-person forms which may have rational or nonrational referents.

A model of the semantic structure of the Kannada pronominal system is presented in figure 2.5 as an ordered series of binary oppositions in the form of a key diagram. The ordering proceeds from universals to particulars and, among particulars, attempts to express the semantic relations among the pronominal sets by showing simply and economically the neutralizations through which they are related. Four Kannada pronouns may be defined by the combinations of semantic features from the universal dimensions of person and number. Three more oppositions are required to distinguish among the remaining pronouns, whose definitions include the features $\overline{\text{SA}}$. These will be ordered according to the neutralizations which occur in the person-number suf-

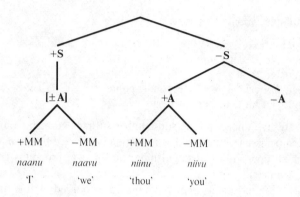

Figure 2.5

fixes of tensed verbs, the person-number suffixes of the imperatives, and the interrogative pronouns.

As was noted, Kannada nouns fall into two classes, rational and nonrational. The interrogative pronouns *yaaru* 'who' and *yaavadu* 'which one' reveal that this opposition is relevant though implicit in most of the pronominal system, since speaker and addressee are by definition members of the rational category. For this reason the feature 'rational' (in parenthesis where it is redundant) is inserted immediately after the person features and just before the opposition ±minimal membership. Only nouns in the rational class designate beings that are either male or female. Therefore within the rational class, there is an opposition of male (♂) vs. female (♀). This opposition is not contrastive in first person forms. In second person forms, it is contrastive only in the imperatives with vocative clitics. In the third person, it is contrastive in all singular forms.

The sixth and last opposition of distance, close and remote, occurs only in third-person independent pronouns (i.e., in none of the person-number suffixes). This opposition is represented as close (c) and remote (r) in figure 2.6 which displays, in the form of a key, the Kannada person system beginning with universal oppositions and adding those needed to distinguish Kannada person forms from each other, ordered to show the neutralizations through which one set of person markers is related to another. Three pronominal forms have a second meaning: *niivu* 'you' and 'thou polite'; *ivaru* 'they close' and 'he/she close, polite'; *avaru* 'they remote' and 'he/she remote, polite'. In each case

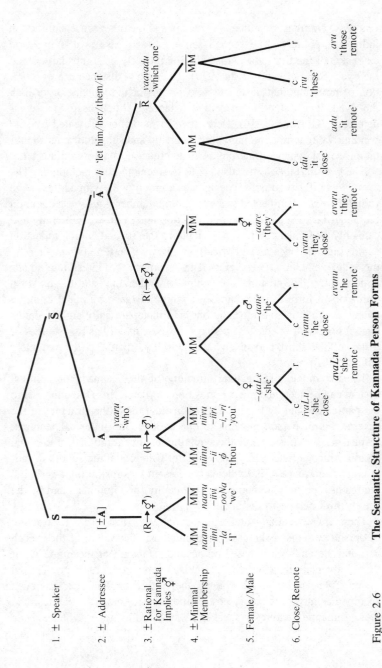

1. ± Speaker

2. ± Addressee

3. ± Rational for Kannada Implies ♂

4. ± Minimal Membership

5. Female/Male

6. Close/Remote

Figure 2.6   **The Semantic Structure of Kannada Person Forms**

one sense signifies more than one person and the other sense signifies an individual politely. The second sense in each case is a metaphoric extension of the first. Social distance is a property of groups larger than the dyad (Simmel 1950, Bean 1970). Thus social distance is a connotation of pronouns that designate associations of individuals larger than the dyad. The enlarging of social distance is often used to express deference (Goffman 1956). Here, then, a metaphor is created by suspending the feature nonminimal membership and substituting its connotation, social distance (interpreted as deference), as a criterial attribute.

The two marginal forms also are to be understood as metaphors. The form *niivugaLu* 'you polite' designates a group politely in address. The form *niivugaLu* is inflected twice for plural number (*-gaLu* is a common plural suffix). The double plural inflection makes no sense literally and can only be understood as a metaphor, the second plural inflection signifying deference metaphorically as above. The term *taavu*, literally the reflexive 'themselves', is used in Avaruuru to address individuals honorifically. The feature 'nonminimal membership' and the use of a third-person form to the addressee connote distance by transforming a dyadic interaction into a triadic one and metaphorically signify deference for the addressee. It is, perhaps, because *taavu* has two sources of distance, the third person and the plurality, that it is an extremely deferential form.

Thus, a model of semantic structure of the Kannada pronominal system can be specified in six oppositions, ordered from the universal to the particular, and by the neutralizations that relate the structure of the several sets of person markers to one another: the indexical features, $\pm$speaker, $\pm$addressee, and the symbolic features $\pm$rational, $\pm$minimal membership, female/male, close/remote. Deferential metaphors for address and reference to individuals are created by substituting as criterial the feature 'politely' connoted by the feature 'nonminimal', and by the use of third-person forms in address.

There are several advantages to this analysis. The semantic structure of person systems is shown to be grounded in the nature of the speech act, and the analysis is based on an understanding of the influence of these universal characteristics on the semantic structure of pronominal systems. The unity of the domain, heretofore unidentified, has been specified as the combinatory possibilities of two semantic features, and these semantic features, 'speaker' **S** and 'addressee' **A**, have been shown to be indexical rather than symbolic. Finally, the particular char-

acteristics of the system are accounted for by including all person forms
(not just independent pronouns) so that the semantic relationships
among the several sets of person forms are ordered by a hierarchy of
neutralizations.

The Second-Person Forms in Context

Many Kannada verbs are obligatorily marked for the person and number of their subject; for example:

> the nonpast tense, *hoogtiini* 'I go', 'I will go'
> the past tense, *hoode* 'I went'
> the imperative, *hoogu* 'go thou'.

In such cases the inclusion of an independent subject pronoun is optional. For example, in the sentences

> *niinu hoogtiiya* 'will thou go'
> *niinu hoode* 'thou went',

the pronoun *niinu* 'thou, you-sg.' is optional, since the verb already carries a second-person singular suffix (*-ii-*, *-e*). Other Kannada verb forms have no person-number suffix:

> conditional *hoodre* 'if ——— go'
> negative *hoogalla* '———not going'.

In utterances with verb forms having no person-number suffix, a subject pronoun is obligatory unless the subject is clear from the social or linguistic context. Further, some Kannada sentences contain no verb form. In such utterances a pronoun usually occurs:

> *yaara huDagi niinu* 'whose girl (are) you sg.'
> *niinu mudaki* 'you-sg. (are) an old woman'.

In sentences which include both a verb with a

person-number suffix and a subject pronoun, the redundant pronoun usually occurs for focus or emphasis:

niinu hoogtiiya 'will you-sg. go?'
niinee hoogtiiya 'will you-sg.-emphatic go?'

If the second person is not the subject of the verb, the pronoun, now in an oblique case, is obligatory:

nindu nanka koDu 'yours-sg. to me give'
ninku illa makkaLu 'for you-sg. no children', i.e., 'you have no
  children'
nimge koTTru 'to you-pl. they gave'
nimge yešTu sambLa barutte 'to you-pl. how much salary comes'.

It is important to note that first- and second-person subjects and objects of verbs may only be expressed by person forms, while third-person subjects and objects of verbs may be expressed either by person forms or by nouns. In the sentence *naanu hoogtiini* 'I go', *naanu* and *-iini* 'first person singular' cannot be replaced by noun such as **lakšmamma hoogtiini* 'I, Lakšmamma, go'. Similarly, in *ninage koDutiini* 'I give to you', *ninage* 'to you' and *-iini* 'I' cannot be replaced by a noun such as **akkange koDutiini* in the sense 'I give to you, elder sister'. Thus first- and second-person subjects and objects are always pronouns or person suffixes. By contrast, third-person subjects and objects of verbs may be nouns or pronouns:

avanu hoogtaane 'he goes', or
raama hoogtaane 'Rama goes'
avanige koDu 'give to him', or
aNNange koDu 'give to elder brother'.

Nouns are not shifters. Therefore, like third-person pronouns, subject nouns signify persons or objects not participating in the speech event. In Kannada, nouns never function as first- or second-person subjects or objects of verbs. However, they may function as vocatives, calling attention to the addressee. (Vocatives are not subjects or objects of verbs.) Thus second-person forms not only indicate the addressee as do vocative nouns; they also enable a message to be about its recipient, which vocative nouns do not. For example, in the utterance, *uuTa koDu* 'give dinner', the verb form is a second-person singular imperative (*koDu*). As a second-person shifter, it indicates its recipient, but in addition it is part of a message about the recipient, telling him to 'give dinner'. Similarly, in the utterance *ninage koTTra* 'did they give to you?', the pronoun *ninage* 'to you' both indicates its recipient and refers to the recipient's role in the narrated event as the possible receiver of something. Vocative nouns (kinship terms, status terms, and personal names), on the other hand, can only indicate the recipient; they cannot at the same time refer to his role, if any, in the narrated event. For example, in the utterance *akka yaarige koTTru* 'elder sister, to whom did they give (it)', 'elder sister' is the recipient of the message indicated by the vocative *akka,* but the narrated event is about others ('to whom' and 'they'). In order to express a message that is both directed at 'elder sister' and about 'elder sister', person forms must be used, for example, *akka, ninage koTTra* 'elder sister, to you did they give?'

Thus, in Kannada, the addressee or second person may be indicated by second-person forms (pronouns and person suffixes) and vocative nouns. Of these, only the pronouns and person suffixes signify the role of the addressee in the narrated event: the pronouns function either as subjects or objects of verbs; the person suffixes only as subjects.

Social Context

In chapter 2 definitions of the person pronouns and suffixes in Kannada were given in terms of semantic oppositions ordered according to their universality and by the semantic relationships between sets of person forms. The forms and definitions of second-person forms are reviewed and reorganized in table 3.1 to facilitate the discussion of their use. The semantic features occurring in the definitions are **S** = speaker, **A** = addressee, MM = minimal relationship, sr = socially remote, and sc = socially close (see appendix 1 for notation list).

Some of the forms in different classes in the table are synonymous, that is, they have the same definitions. There are five distinct definitions:

1. $\overline{S}$.A.MM
2. $\overline{S}$.A.MM.sr
3. $\overline{S}$.A.MM.sr,sr
4. $\overline{S}$.A.$\overline{MM}$
5. $\overline{S}$.A.$\overline{MM}$.sr

In addition, the vocative suffixes *-ee, -gee,* and *-oo,* mentioned in the

Table 3.1   **Second Person Forms**

Class	Form	Gloss	Definition
Pronouns	*niinu*	'thou'	$\overline{S}$.A.$\overline{MM}$
	niivu	a. 'you'	$\overline{S}$.A.$\overline{MM}$
		b. 'thou, polite'	$\overline{S}$.A.$\overline{MM}$.sr
	niivugaLu	'you, polite'	$\overline{S}$.A.$\overline{MM}$.sr
	taavu	'thou, honorific'	$\overline{S}$.A.$\overline{MM}$.sr.sr
Verbal Suffixes	*-ii, -iiya*	'thou'	$\overline{S}$.A.$\overline{MM}$
	-iiri, -ri, -ra	a. 'you'	$\overline{S}$.A.$\overline{MM}$
		b. 'thou, polite'	$\overline{S}$.A.$\overline{MM}$.sr
Imperatives	ø (form identical with verb root)	'thou'	$\overline{S}$.A.$\overline{MM}$
	-i, -ri	a. 'you'	$\overline{S}$.A.$\overline{MM}$
		b. 'thou, polite'	$\overline{S}$.A.$\overline{MM}$.sr

previous chapter, may be added to the singular imperative (definition 1), thereby introducing additional discriminations among the social identities of individual addresses.

Of the second-person forms which may be used to address a group, there are two independent pronouns, one imperative, and one verbal suffix. Therefore, no distinctions among the social identities of groups of addressees or their relations to the speaker can be communicated by the verb form alone. Of the two pronouns *niivu* 'you-pl.' and *niivugaLu* 'you-pl. polite', the form *niivugaLu* 'you polite' occurs rarely and is formally aberrant, since it is marked twice for plural number (*-vu* and *-gaLu*). The pronoun *niivugaLu* was reported by a number of informants as a polite form for addressing a group, but it was heard only rarely for addressing high-status outsiders such as government officials. In effect, then, the pronoun *niivu* 'you' and the plural imperative and plural second-person suffix are the only second-person forms for a group of addressees.

Second-person forms used to individuals are greater in number and more varied in the distinctions of social identity expressed. This abundance of terms for an individual addressee is typical of the Kannada system as a whole, and is apparently a common phenomenon in address systems (certainly it is true of English), probably because a group of addressees may be composed of individuals of very different social status, and, more fundamentally, because most speech acts are dyadic (see chapter 1).

The most widely occurring second-person forms for individual addressees are the second-person singular pronoun (*niinu*), the imperative
singular (identical in form with the verb root), and the singular verbal
suffixes. These were used in the village at one time or another by
everyone to anyone else. For example:

> *koDu* 'give (the shovel)' a high-ranking Kuruba landowner to a
> low-ranking A.K. laborer;
> *hoogtiiya* 'will you-sg. go?' an A.K. man to a Kuruba man;
> *illee kuutidiya* 'right-here have-you-sg.-sat?' an A.K. woman to a
> Kuruba man;
> *yeen, kelasa maaDtiiya* 'well, will-you (do) work?' a Kuruba
> woman to her husband;
> *uuTa maaDi hoogu* 'eat food and go-sg.' Kuruba mother to her son.
> *uuTa maaDu* 'have-sg. dinner' a daughter to her mother, father,
> elder brother or elder sister.
> *yelli iddiiya* 'where are-you-sg.' people to goddess Maari during a
> ritual.

Among kinsmen these singular second-person forms are used almost
exclusively, although a younger kinsman is likely to omit the pronoun
(*niinu*) and to use instead the appropriate kinship term (see chapter 5).
Husbands and wives use the singular forms to each other, but the wife
also uses plural forms, and the husband uses singular forms with the *-ee*
vocative suffix (to be discussed below). Second-person singular forms
may be made more polite or deferential by the addition of one of several
kinship terms: *amma* literally 'mother', *appa* literally 'father', *aNNa*
literally 'elder brother', and *akka* literally 'elder sister' occur metaphorically in polite address to non-kin; *taayi* literally 'mother' is also used to
address to nonkin. The nonkin status term *svaami* 'lord, sir' may also
occur with second person singular verbs. (The latter four terms, *aNNa,
akka, taayi, svaami,* may occur with plural verb forms as well.) The
singular pronouns, verbal suffixes, and imperatives, then, are the basic
second-person forms, acceptable in at least some circumstances for any
fellow villager.

Intimate Usages

One singular second-person form, the imperative verb, can be modified
by the addition of vocative suffixes: *-oo, -ee, -gee, -l̄ee*. These forms are
restricted by definition to particular classes of addressees. It will be-

come clear in the following discussion that *-oo* may be glossed 'socially
close male', *-ee* 'socially close female' *-lee* 'emphatic', and *-gee* 'emphatic used only by A.K.s'.

In the village all little boys (until the age of about twelve) may be
addressed with a singular imperative verb with the *-oo* vocative suffix
by adults of all castes and both sexes. They may also be addressed with
the singular imperative or the imperative with *-appa* attached (see chapter 5). Thus, for example, *baaroo, baa, baappa* (from *baa* 'come') are
all possible. Little boys are almost always addressed by their playmates
with the *-oo* suffix. As they grow up, male playmates, who are usually
of the same or similarly ranked caste, continue to use the *-oo* vocative to
each other, often for the rest of their lives. Similarly, men continue to
receive the *-oo* vocative suffix from older men who have known them
since childhood. It is possible for a younger man to use the *-oo* suffix to
an older one if the two are on especially good terms, (*višvaasa cen-
naagidre* 'from affection'). Women tend to drop the *-oo* suffix as their
male childhood playmates or younger male kinsmen reach adulthood.
The *-oo* forms are replaced by the singular imperative alone or with the
form *appa* attached. This change in usage for women may be partly due
to the fact that at marriage a woman moves to her husband's house,
leaving her childhood playmates behind to be visited only occasionally.
She acquires, for everyday contact, her husband's relatives and
neighbors, with whom she may be only recently acquainted. Primarily,
however, the change in usage is an expression of the higher status of
adult men in the society. Consequently, men are in general entitled to
deferential treatment from women.

Thus, age, sex, and closeness are important factors in selecting the
-oo suffix. Futhermore, all men of the untouchable A.K. jaati are addressed with the *-oo* suffix by men and boys of all other castes. (Women
do not follow this usage.) Here a difference in caste rank is expressed
through the patterns of use of this vocative suffix. Members of the A.K.
jaati, the only untouchable (ritually polluting) caste in the village, are
distinguished from members of all other castes.

In addition, many men report a contrast between their usage and that
followed in the nearby city of Bangalore (which may or may not be
accurate). There, they say, only very close friends address each other
with the *-oo* vocative suffix, and the usage is reciprocal.

Inappropriate uses of the *-oo* suffix were occasionally reported. The
village accountant (*šaanboog*), a Brahmin who lives in a nearby town,

addressed one of the village men of a landowning Kuruba family with the *-oo* suffix. This was considered rude and abusive by the man and his family. During a heated argument an A.K. woman addressed a younger Kuruba man with the *-oo* imperative form to express her dissatisfaction with his behavior (something she would never do in more normal circumstances). One young Kuruba man reported that he did not want his slightly older brother to address him with the *-oo* imperative, even though this is commonly acceptable usage. Both he and his elder brother visited the city often and were strongly influenced by city styles (for example, dressing in city style even when in the village). In the city, *-oo* imperatives are reportedly used only among close male friends. Moreover, the younger brother does not consider himself socially subordinate to his elder brother, despite the age difference, since he holds a good job at a factory and earns one of the highest salaries in the village.

The *-oo* imperative, then, is used only to males, but not to every male. It is used to males who are younger or of lower status, or to males with whom one is on especially good terms, usually resulting from long and intimate acquaintance. It is possible to extract a common element from usage to juniors in age or status, and to intimates. These are all people to whom the speaker is permitted to get close. When the closeness is reciprocal, it is that of intimacy; when it is nonreciprocal (e.g., to a junior who replies with some other form), it is an expression of a power or status difference in which only the superior may approach the personal sphere of his subordinate. Thus the *-oo* suffix may be glossed 'socially close male'. The social variables considered by a speaker in deciding if his addressee may be given a term that signifies closeness, are age, generally a distinction between child and adult status; closeness of acquaintance (childhood playmates and men who have been acquainted since childhood are likely to find reciprocal or nonreciprocal use of *-oo* appropriate); caste rank, men of the A.K. jaati being distinguished from the others (middle ranking non-Brahmin castes). In addition, some villagers explicitly recognize distinctions between village and city usage.

The occurrence of the vocative suffix *-ee* 'socially close female' is in some respects parallel to that of the *-oo* suffix 'close male' and in some respects distinct. It signifies a female rather than a male addressee, but the rules for its use are somewhat different. Imperative verbs with *-ee* are used among little girls (prepuberty) who are playmates. The *-ee* form is used by adult women to little girls, especially close kinsmen such as daughter, brother's daughter, and husband's brother's daughter. It is somewhat less appropriate for the children of others, who, one informant reported, should be addressed *baamma* 'come amma', that is, with the *amma* form, a more polite usage than the imperative alone or the imperative with the *-ee* suffix. Adult women who are close in age and status use the *-ee* form among themselves. Older adult women also use *-ee* forms to their grown daughters, daughters-in-law, and other close junior kinswomen. The *-ee* imperatives are not used to women older than the speaker, except occasionally by women of middle-ranking castes to A.K. women. A.K. women report that they never use *-ee* imperatives to women of other castes.[1]

Men may use the imperative with *-ee* only to their wives and to unmarried junior female cross-cousins, or elder sister's daughters, who are preferred potential wives. A woman's husband would get angry if this usage were to continue after marriage. While it is possible for a man to use the *-ee* imperative to a potential wife, in fact, the usage is rare, for it would make the young man and his potential wife the focus of enthusiastic teasing and cause embarrassment to both of them. The only time the *-ee* imperative is used in this way is among small children who like to play wedding. During one such celebration the six-year-old 'bridegroom' called to his somewhat younger cross-cousin: *baaree maduve aag* . . . (the rest was lost) 'come (+-*ee*) the wedding (will) take place'.

This restriction on the use of *-ee* imperatives to actual or potential wives is apparently limited in distribution. All castes in the village follow this usage but are aware of different customs elsewhere. The father of a woman married into the village from a place about fifteen miles away addressed his daughter with *-ee* imperatives. The people who reported this commented that it sounded peculiar to them. Others reported that men in Mysore City to the south and Cikballapura to the north also use *-ee* imperatives to their daughters. Thus the people of Avaruuru are aware of different customs in other places; and that, while in Avaruuru the 'close female' signification of the *-ee* feminine vocative suffix strongly connotes an actual or potential sexual intimacy between a male speaker and the addressee, in other places it does not.

A number of people commented that the *-ee* vocatives are *haLLi baaše* 'village language' and *cennaagilla* 'not nice'. They said that city men and educated men do not use these forms to their wives; instead they use the imperative alone (e.g., *baa* 'come') or even the polite imperative (e.g., *banni* 'come polite'). Men with strong ties to the city and "enlightened" (educated) manners reported the latter usage for themselves and their friends. Several children said that their fathers used *-ee* forms to their mothers most often when angry at them. (Men never use the imperative with *amma*, literally 'mother', to their wives because of an incestuous connotation [Bean 1975b].)

Several inappropriate uses of *-ee* imperatives were noted. Little girls occasionally use *-ee* vocatives to their mothers. One little girl who reported this usage for herself was proud and gleeful at her brazenness. Others were a bit more sober, reporting that such a thing might happen, but that a mother would certainly spank a daughter who spoke to her that way. On one occasion a woman was heard calling to her son: *baamma baaree* 'come *amma* come + *-ee*', which may be glossed 'come woman (politely), come socially close female'. She was reprimanding him for not looking after his younger brother as he was supposed to. The mother was shaming her son by addressing him as if he were a girl.

Thus *-ee* is glossed 'close female'. It signifies a female addressee to whom the speaker may get close. The sociocultural categories that are relevant for the speaker's decision that closeness may be expressed are the same as those relevant for the selection of *-oo* imperatives: age, untouchable-caste membership, closeness of acquaintance. The major difference is that the closeness signified by *-ee* has a strong connotation of sexuality and is properly used by men only to their wives or unmarried potential wives. Villagers are aware not only of differences between city usage and village usage, but of geographical distribution of usage, and they tend to judge city usage as superior or learned, and village usage as crude or unsophisticated.

The vocative clitic *-lee* may be added for emphasis to the imperatives with *-ee* or *-oo* and to some vocative nouns (e.g., *appalee* 'father, emphatic vocative'; *ammalee* 'mother, emphatic vocative'; *hoogolee* 'go, close male emphatic'; *hoogelee* 'go, close female emphatic'). This emphatic vocative suffix is used in the same way as the vocative suffixes already discussed and evokes no further discriminations in the social identity of speaker and addressee and the relationship between them. However, there is another emphatic vocative clitic, *-gee,* which occurs after singular imperatives with or without *-ee*, after *amma* 'mother', and after interrogatives (e.g., *yeenegee* 'what' and *yaakegee* 'why'). It is used in much the same way as the *-ee* imperative, except that this form is used only by A.K.s to women necessarily of their own caste, since it is a rather insistent emphatic vocative that would be inappropriate to a superior. A Kuruba woman discussing this form remarked: *naavu heeLidre maadigaru antaare* 'if we say (it), they will call us Maadigaru (A.K.s)'. The form *-gee* signifies that *-gee* is a form used only by A.K.s. That is, it signifies an existential association with a class of speakers. It is therefore a form with pragmatic meaning and may be defined by the symbolic feature 'emphatic' and the indexical features 'existentially associated with the addressee', 'spoken only by A.K.s' **AK.**

Deferential Usages

Plural second-person forms are used metaphorically to address an individual. The basis of this metaphor was described in the preceding chapter. Of the plural second-person forms, the pronoun *niivu* 'you, or thou polite' occurs least often, since it is usually omitted in favor of a vocative noun such as a kinship term or a special form of a personal name. The plural/polite imperative has two forms, one ending in *-i* and the other in *-ri* (e.g., *koDi* or *koDri* 'give pl./polite' *hoogi* or *hoogri* 'go pl./polite'). The *-ri* imperative occurs more frequently in village speech.

These second-person plural/polite forms are reported to be the proper address forms for a woman to her husband (although most wives often use the singular imperative, sometimes with the kinship term *maama* 'MB, elder male cross-cousin'—women never address their husbands by name). Second person plural/polite forms are also used by A.K. laborers to their landlords. Further, any senior kinsman may be addressed with the polite imperative, but the ones who most frequently receive these are distant kinsmen and affines. Thus a man or a woman may address his or her spouse's father and mother *barri maama, barri atte* 'come-polite father-in-law, come-polite mother-in-law'. Distant kinsmen, if older than the speaker, may be addressed *barri akka, barri aNNa* 'come-polite elder sister, come-polite elder brother'. In these cases the singular imperative is also possible, and the use of the plural/ polite may be compared with the addition of 'please' in English, for which there is no similarly used lexeme in Kannada.

People in positions of power regularly receive polite imperatives from those subject to their power. A boss at work, for example, may be addressed with the polite imperative and a vocative pronoun *avare* attached (see chapter 7), *svaami* 'lord, sir', or *govDa* 'landlord'. Thus an A.K. woman addressing a man from an important landowning Kuruba household, especially if she wants something, may say *govDa barri* 'landlord, (please) come'. High status outsiders like an-thropologists, doctors, and government officials are likely to receive the plural/polite.

Plural/polite second-person forms occur much less often than singular forms in village speech among the village residents. People who are influenced by city styles and who are educated report that polite impera-tives are better forms for addressing one's acquaintances. Some men even claim to address their wives with a polite imperative, a usage that was never observed. In any case, those villagers who are aware of city styles are likely to have a much greater frequency of plural/polite forms in their speech.

The verbs that most often occur in the polite imperative are *barri* 'come, polite', *hoogri* 'go, polite', *koDri* 'give, polite', *kuutkoLLri* 'sit, polite', and *uuTa maaDri* 'have dinner, polite'. These are to be under-stood not as orders, but as requests or invitations. The glosses might include the word 'please'. When an invitation or request is made of anyone, these forms may be used. They are used in this way to people of lower status and to children. Similarly, second-person plural suffixes occur on verbs used to address individuals whenever the speaker wishes to be a bit more polite. For example, a daughter is asked to do an errand: *eema ciici heeLtiira* 'eema, will you (please) tell your father's younger brother's wife?'

There are a few contexts in the village in which plural/polite verb-forms occur more frequently than singular ones. When A.K.s ask their patrons a question, they are likely to use the plural/polite forms. Moreover, since they usually go to their patrons when they want some-thing, the extra politeness of these forms is especially appropriate.

> *yeen cikkaNNa tooTak hoogtiiri* 'well, cikkaNNa, are you-polite going to the garden?'
> *svaami koDutiira* 'lord, will you-polite give?'
> *muniyeŋTappanavare yelli hoogtiira, koTTbiTThoogri*
> 'muniyeŋTappa sir, where are you-polite going, please go only after having given'.

Singular verbs can occur in the first two examples but are less deferen-tial. Women are likely to address questions to their husbands with a plural/polite form, especially when the question has some other func-tion, such as a greeting when the husband comes home: *yelli hoogiddri* 'where have you-polite been'.

Thus the plural person forms, pronouns, imperatives, and person-number suffixes occur in two distinct circumstances in village speech. In the first, they are used to make polite inquiries, requests, and invitations. As such, they may be used by speakers to addressees of any rank or status. Their use depends on the function of the utterance rather than the social identities of speaker and addressee. In the second, it is the social identities of speaker and addressee that are significant. Usually in the village a second-person plural/polite form is used nonreciprocally to express a power difference. The only addressees in the village who regularly receive plural/polite forms are husbands from their wives, and landlords from their laborers. Both relationships are supposed to be clothed in the behavior of master and servant. It is only among educated persons with strong city ties that plural/polite forms are used reciprocally, for example, between acquaintances. Plural/polite forms, then, are used by the speaker to show deference to addressees who are considerably more powerful than he, or to those of whom he is making an especially polite request. In either case deference is expressed by the social distance created metaphorically in the use of a plural form to an individual addressee.

Definitions and Selection Criteria

Three classes of second-person forms have been discussed: pronouns, person suffixes on verbs, and vocative suffixes on imperative verbs. Some terms from each formal class have the same significata (i.e., are synonymous), and the discussion in this chapter was based on the classification according to definition rather than form.

The forms for individual addressees are more varied. Including among these the singular imperatives, *-ee* 'close female', *-oo* 'close male', and *-gee* 'form used by A.K.s only', three semantic classes emerge:

1. singular second-person forms defined: $\overline{\text{S}}$.A.MM
2. singular imperatives with vocative suffixes: $\overline{\text{S}}$.A.MM.sc. $\male$/$\female$. $\pm$**AK**
3. plural/polite person forms: **S.A.MM.sr**

(**S** = speaker, **A** = addressee, MM = minimal membership, sc = socially close, sr = socially remote, $\male$ = male, $\female$ = female, and **AK** = form uttered by A.K.s only.)

These classes contrast on the basis of social distance. The forms in class 1 are not marked for social distance and often occur in the same contexts as forms from classes 2 and 3. By contrast, forms from classes 2 and 3 are marked for social distance, class 2 being 'socially close' and class 3 'socially remote': the speaker when using these forms always expresses closeness or distance between himself and the addressee. The *niinu* class in opposition to the *-ee* class is polite, while in contrast to the *niivu* class it is familiar. The relationship between terms in these opposed classes that of unmarked to marked (fig. 3.1).The unmarked class

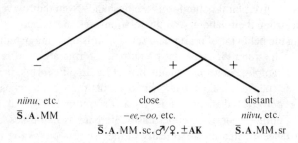

niinu, etc.	close	distant
S̄.A.MM	*−ee,−oo*, etc.	*niivu*, etc.
	S̄.A.MM.sc.♂/♀.±AK	S̄.A.MM.sr

Figure 3.1

(*niinu* 'thou', etc.) has no distinction of social distance. It is possible for a speaker to use niinu 'thou' where *niivu* 'you' might be more appropriate without appearing rude. As one villager put it: *baa cenaagide banni tumba cenda* '*baa* (singular imperative) is nice, *banni* (plural/polite imperative) is very nice'. Thus *baa* is all right, but by contrast *banni* is more polite and *baaree* more familiar. The two marked classes have metalinguistic lexical labels and are the subject of discussion among villagers. The class of 'socially close' terms is called *yeekavacana*, literally 'singular', but metaphorically 'intimate', while the class of 'socially remote' terms are *bahuvacana*, literally 'plural', but metaphorically 'deferential' (for fuller explication see Bean 1974a). Illustrating this relationship, one villager said that *baa* 'come-singular' (unmarked) is neither *yeekavacana* 'familiar speech' nor *bahuvacana* 'deferential speech'.

When a speaker selects a form from among these three semantic classes, his decision is based on an evaluation of the relationship of the addressee to himself, which is dependent on the relative social identities of speaker and addressee. It is on this basis that he decides if a form having the meaning 'socially close' or one having the meaning 'socially remote' is appropriate. From the discussion of the ways in which these terms are used by villagers, several sociocultural categories emerge as significant for this decision:

1. *Age*. Children were almost always the recipients of 'socially close' forms, indicating the importance of a distinction between child and adult.

2. *Caste rank*. A number of forms were considered appropriate for use to or by A.K.s, thus differentiating them from the other castes in the village and setting up a significant distinction between touchable and untouchable castes.

3. *Socioeconomic status*. Landlords, heads of landowning house-holds, frequently received nonreciprocal 'socially remote' forms from their agricultural and house servants and occasionally from others. Their power as landowners makes them the political and economic leaders of the village. On account of this they are entitled to deference, and on account of this they are the chief granters of requests and givers of goods and services. It is their duty to give and the right of others, less fortunate, to ask.

4. *Husband and wife*. This is the only intracaste relationship in which distant forms are expected to be given regularly by one party (the wife) and close forms by the other party (the husband). Distant forms may be given visiting affines and distant relatives but here it is more a function of the formal hospitality due them than of their superior status. The relationship between husband and wife is unique.

The four sociocultural categories so far discussed are those which create status differentials between speaker and addressee such that if the speaker gives a close or neutral term, he expects to receive a remote one, or if he gives a remote or neutral term, he expects to receive a close one. That is, the usage is nonreciprocal and constitutes what Brown and Gilman (1960) called the power semantic—the power difference is symbolized in the nonreciprocal use of person forms, the superior using close or neutral terms and expecting to receive a neutral or remote term for his close one, or a distant one for his neutral term. Thus, a husband may say *baa* or *baaree* to his wife, and she may say *baa* or *barri* to him.

5. *The length and intimacy of acquaintance*. If the addressee and speaker are of relatively equal age and status and know each other well (this factor is taken into consideration after those which yield power differentials), they will exchange close forms. If they are of relatively

equal status but differ significantly in age and have known each other for a long time (e.g., an old man to his brother's son), the elder is likely to give close forms but will, of course, not receive them.

6. *Function of the utterance.* This factor is not directly related to the social identities of speaker and addressee, but to the illocutionary force of the utterance. When the speaker is issuing an invitation, or making a polite inquiry or request, he is likely to use distant forms to express the politeness of his request.

7. *Local usage.* Finally, villagers are aware that their customs differ from those of people in other parts of the Kannada-speaking area and from those of people who live in the city. Some tend to emulate city speech styles, others merely make note of them as they make note of different usages in other villages.

The rules of usage discussed in this chapter are least elaborate for the unmarked forms (*niinu,* etc.) which only communicate that the addressee is the addressee. The marked forms are more restricted in use (and therefore more discussed by villagers), since these express not only that the addressee is the addressee, but also that the speaker is socially close to, or distant from, the addressee. In these cases, as we would expect, there are explicit rules about what sorts of speakers, for the purposes of what kinds of communication, express closeness to, or distance from what kinds of addressees.

4 The Semantic Structure of the Kannada System of Kin Classification

Kannada Kinship Terminology

Kinship terms occupy an important place in the Kannada system of address. They occur frequently, not only in their central genealogical senses, but also as the designations of wider classes of kinsmen, and metaphorically in address to nonkin. Further, kinship terms regularly occur in address as parts of personal names (see chapter 7) and they often occur with second person verb forms (see chapter 3). Their frequency, polysemy, and combination with other second-person forms in address make kinship terms a large and complex part of the address system (and a rich source of its variation).

Although only the senior members of reciprocal sets of kinship terms occur in address, it is necessary to consider the kin classification system as a whole, because the meanings of kinship terms that occur in address are in part dependent on their relationships to other terms in the total system. Therefore an analysis of the semantic structure of the system of kin classification is a necessary prerequisite to the elucidation of the meanings of kinship terms in address.

The goal of the analysis that follows is to provide definitions of the kinship terms in both their focal and widest senses. These definitions form the basis for analysis of and comparison with the data on kinship terms of address in their primary, widened, and metaphoric senses. The analysis begins by establish-

ing focal kintypes for each term, and by specifying a componential
definition for each term in its primary sense (as it is used to designate its
focal kin class). The broader ranges of denotata are then considered. In
order to give definitions of these wider classes, the basis on which they
are constituted must be specified. Therefore a set of equivalence rules is
formulated to account for the extension of the terms from their focal to
their nonfocal denotata. The equivalence rules reflect the neutralizations
of genealogical oppositions (such as lineal v. collateral) on which the
extensions from focal kintypes (such as 'grandfather') to more distant
denotata (such as 'grandfather's brother') are based. Thus the set of
equivalence rules serves to specify the semantic structure of the wider
kin classes. Finally, having established the primary sense of each term,
and having specified the relationships among its denotata, componential
definitions of each term in its widest sense are given.[1]

The Kannada system of kin classification is typologically Dravidian
(Dumont 1953, Scheffler 1971).[2] Dravidian systems terminologically
distinguish kin classes that include cross-collateral kinsmen from those
that include lineal and parallel-collateral kinsmen. Membership in
'cross' and 'noncross' classes is extended to more distant collaterals
according to the relative sexes (same or different) of the linking
kinsmen. Further, in this variety of Dravidian system, there is no separate set of terms for in-laws. Relatives by marriage are included in the
cross and noncross kin classes. Finally, the several classes of 'cross'
and 'noncross' kinsmen are distinguished from one another on the basis
of the sex and generation of the designated kinsman, and additionally,
for some kin classes, the sex of the propositus and the relative age
within the generation of the designated kinsman. (For similar Dravidian
systems, see for example Beck 1972, Karve 1968, Dumont 1957, Tyler
1969.)

When Kannada speakers in Avaruuru wish to inquire about or discuss
relationships of genealogical connection or marriage, they do so using a
particular construction. The corpus of kinship terms may be elicited in
this frame.[3] Two examples of these expressions are given below, followed by explanation and discussion of variations that occur:

>   *avanu nanage tamma aagbeeku* 'he to-me younger-brother related-
>   as'
>   *naanu ninage akka aagbeeku* 'I to-you elder-sister related-as'.

In this frame the propositus and the designated relative are represented

by the two pronouns: the designated relative in the nominative case
(e.g., *avanu* 'he', *naanu* 'I') and the propositus in the dative case (with
the suffix *-ge*; e.g., *nanage* 'to me', *ninage* 'to you'). The kinship term
(e.g., *tamma* 'younger brother', *akka* 'elder sister') also occurs in the
nominative case. The verb form *aagbeeku* is a compound consisting
of *aag-* the verb stem meaning 'happen, occur, become' and *beeku* a
modal meaning 'ought to, should, must'. Variations of this construction, in which parts of it are deleted, are possible:

avanu tamma 'he (is) younger-brother'
avanu nanage tamma 'he to-me (is) younger-brother'
nanage tamma 'to-me younger-brother'
tamma aagbeeku 'younger-brother related-as'.

This frame almost always describes a kin relationship. Occasionally,
however, the frame is used metaphorically; for example:

namage sneetaru aagbeeku 'to-us friends related-as'
akkan aagbeeku koDutaaLe 'elder-sister related-as, she will give'.

In the first case, the nonkin meaning is obvious from the meaning of
sneetaru 'friends', which refers to individuals who are intimate, but not
kinsmen. In the second case, the social setting in which the phrase is
spoken may clearly indicate that *akka* 'elder sister' is not a kinsman—if,
for example, the speaker is of one caste and the referent of another.
However, if the kinship status of the referent remains unclear to the
hearer, he may resolve the ambiguity by asking, as a speaker did on one
occasion, using the *aagbeeku* frame: *yeen aagbeeku* 'what related-as';
and on that occasion the first speaker replied: *yeenu illa, avaru beere*
'nothing they (are) different', thereby revealing that the *aagbeeku* frame
was used metaphorically in the cases where it was applied to nonkin. In
its nonmetaphorical uses, the *aagbeeku* frame is applied only to relationships of consanguinity and affinity. The terms elicited by this frame
are those used to classify relationships of descent and marriage. A
semantic analysis of the terms and designata elicited by this frame will
yield the structure of the system of kin classification.

The corpus of terms that occur in the *aagbeeku* frame is summarized in
table 4.1. Each expression is given with the focal denotatum and, for
future reference, the definitions of the terms in their primary and widened senses.

Table 4.1 **Kin Terms and Definitions** (See Appendix 1 for Notations)

Term	Focal Kintype	Primary Sense	Expanded Sense
muttaata	PPF	K.G^{+3}.L.♂	K.G^{+3}.♂
muttajji	PPM	K.G^{+3}.L.♀	K.G^{+3}.♀
mumaga	CCS	K.G^{-3}.L.♂	K.G^{-3}.♂
mumagaLu	CCD	K.G^{-3}.L.♀	K.G^{-3}.♀
taata	PF	K.G^{+2}.L.♂	K.G^{+2}.♂
ajji, ammaNNi	PM	K.G^{+2}.L.♀	K.G^{+2}.♀
momaga	CS	K.G^{-2}.L.♂	K.G^{-2}.♂
momagaLu	CD	K.G^{-2}.L.♀	K.G^{-2}.♀
tande, appa	F	K.G^{+1}.L.♂	K.G^{+1}.$\bar{X}$.♂
doDDappa	FB+	K.G^{+1}.+.//Co^1.♂	K.G^{+1}.+.$\bar{X}$.♂
cikkappa	FB−	K.G^{+1}.−.//Co^1.♂	K.G^{+1}.−.$\bar{X}$.♂
taayi, amma	M	K.G^{+1}.L.♀	K.G^{+1}.$\bar{X}$.♀
doDDamma	MZ+	K.G^{+1}.+.//Co^1.♀	K.G^{+1}.+.$\bar{X}$.♀
cikkamma	MZ−	K.G^{+1}.−.//Co^1.♀	K.G^{+1}.−.$\bar{X}$.♀
maga	S	K.G^{-1}.L.♂	K.G^{-1}.$\bar{X}$.♂
magaLu	D	K.G^{-1}.L.♀	K.G^{-1}.$\bar{X}$.♀
aNNa	B+	K.G$''$.+.Co-L.♂	K.G$''$.+.$\bar{X}$.♂
akka	Z+	K.G$''$.+.Co-L.♀	K.G$''$.+.$\bar{X}$.♀
tamma	B−	K.G$''$.−.Co-L.♂	K.G$''$.−.$\bar{X}$.♂
tangi	Z−	K.G$''$.−.Co-L.♀	K.G$''$.−.$\bar{X}$.♀
maava	MB	K.G^{+1}.XCo^1.♂	K.G^{+1}.X.♂
atte	FZ	K.G^{+1}.XCo^1.♀	K.G^{+1}.X.♀
aLiya	Sb$_x$S	K.G^{-1}.XCo^1.♂	K.G^{-1}.X.♂
sose	Sb$_x$D	K.G^{-1}.XCo^1.♀	K.G^{-1}.X.♀
baava	PSb$_x$S+	K.G$''$.+.XCo^2.♂	K.G$''$.+.X.♂
attige	PSb$_x$D+	K.G$''$.+.XCo^2.♀	K.G$''$.+.X.♀
maida	PSb$_x$S−♀$_p$	K.G$''$.−.XCo^2.♂.♀$_p$	K.G$''$.−.X.♂.♀$_p$
baamaida	PSb$_x$S−♂$_p$	K.G$''$.−.XCo^2.♂.♂$_p$	K.G$''$.−.X.♂.♂$_p$
naadini	PSb$_x$D−	K.G$''$.−.XCo^2.♀	K.G$''$.−.X.♀

Kin-Class Foci

The focal kin classes were discovered from statements made by informants. Although the conceptualization of focal members of categories and members by extension was not explicitly discussed with informants, such conceptualizations may be inferred from their comments. First of all, villagers regularly talk about close and distant relations. They speak of relations through consanguinity and marriage as *sambanda* 'relation' and of the people so related as *sambandikaru* 'relatives'. These terms are usually used only in the context of relationships by blood or through marriage, but since *sambanda* means merely 'relation', there are occasions on which the term is used to refer to other kinds of relationships, such as friendship or mutual caste membership. Two kinds of *sambanda* are relevant for our present discussion: *duura sambanda* and *rakta sambanda* 'distant relation' and 'blood relation'. These two categories were not offered to me as an opposition by informants, and so I do not present them here as such, but merely as two categories of kinship relations that are frequently mentioned by informants and that demonstrate a way of talking about relationships based on notions of genealogical distance. 'Distant' refers to genealogical distance, people whose relationship is traceable through several generations or ties of marriage. 'Blood', on the other hand, is shared by genealogically close kinsmen; *rakta* 'blood' comes from both parents. However, villagers regularly speak of *rakta sambanda* 'blood relation' only among parents and children, siblings, parents' siblings, siblings' children, and first cousins. The expression *rakta sambanda* is most useful in distinguishing the foci of cross-kin classes because it occurs most often in the context of discussions of marriage preferences. In this society, in which descent is traced patrilineally and people prefer to marry close consanguineal kinsmen, certain kinsmen who are *rakta sambanda* are the preferred marriage partners: first-degree cross-cousins and mother's younger brother–elder sister's daughter. More distant cross-cousins and uncle-niece share less blood and are less preferred as marriage partners. That is, by virtue of having *rakta sambanda,* cross-cousins and uncle-niece are *varše* 'relation', but always in this context 'preferred relation for marriage'.

Another term, *soodara,* is helpful in distinguishing foci. This term usually occurs with labels for kin classes including cross-aunts, -uncles, and parents-in-law (*atte* FZ, *maava* MB); and cross-niece, cross-nephew, and children-in-law (*sose* 'cross-niece' *aLiya* 'cross-nephew'). Often these kin terms are modified so that one hears *soodar maava, soodar atte, soodar sose, soodar aLiya.* The term *soodara* is borrowed from Sanskrit and glossed in dictionaries as 'co-uterine'. In the village it is glossed as *onde hoTTeyinda* 'from the same stomach' or *namma taayi aNNa tammandru, avar kuuDa huTTiroodu, soodara maava* 'my mother's brothers, they who were born together are *soodara maava*'.

In the village, *soodara* occurs only to mark the relationship between first degree cross-aunt and -uncle (although often extended to include their spouses, MBW and FZH) and first degree cross-niece and -nephew, singling out, from the classes of *atte, maava, sose,* and *aLiya,* those who share the most blood (and who are as a consequence preferred marriage partners, parents-in-law, or children-in-law).

Of the terms whose denotata include cross-collateral and affinal relatives, it is the kinsmen who share the most *rakta* 'blood' with the propositus that are the focal members of their respective classes (see table 4.2).

Table 4.2 | **Focal Kin Types (Cross-Classes)**

	♂	♀
G^{+1}	*maava* MB	*atte* FZ
G^{-}	*baava* PSb_xS+	*attige* PSb_xD+
	maida ♀PSb_xS-	*naadini* PSb_xD-
	baamaida ♂PSb_xS-	
G^{-1}	*aLiya* Sb_xS	*sose* Sb_xD

The same principles of blood and genealogical distance are used to distinguish focal from distant members of classes containing lineal and parallel-collateral kinsmen. The adjectives *sonta* 'own' and *satya* 'true' are often used for this purpose: for example, *satya akkanu* 'true elder sister' (born of same parents); *sonta akkanu* 'own elder sister' (born of same parents). These expressions are used primarily with the sibling and child classes, of which the lineal and colineal members are focal.

The relationship among the terms for parents and parents' same-sex siblings also exhibits the focal status of the lineal kinsmen. Of the terms in the corpus, only those for parents (*tande, appa* F; *taayi, amma* M) are not extended to more distant kinsmen. The terms for parents' same-sex siblings, which are extended to more distant kinsmen, consist of the parent terms with the designations *doDD-* 'elder' and *cikk-* 'younger' attached (*doDDappa* FB+, *doDDamma* MZ+, *cikkappa* FB−, *cikkamma* MZ−). The terms for parents and parents' same-sex siblings have the child terms (*maga* S, *magaLu* D) as their common reciprocals. The transparent lexical relationship (i.e., 'mother', 'elder mother', 'younger mother') among these terms and their comembership in a reciprocal set provide evidence that the parent and parent's same-sex sibling terms designate subclasses of a single superclass of which the lineal members M and F are the foci and the collateral members, labeled by the lexically marked terms, are members by extension.

It follows logically that the focal members of the grandparent class are parents of parents, and the true siblings are children of parents (which is also expressed in the use of *satya* 'true' and *sonta* 'own' discussed above). Thus the focal members of the remaining kin classes may be given (table 4.3).

Table 4.3 **Focal Kin Types (Noncross Classes)**

	♂	♀
G^{+3}	*muttaata* 'great grandfather'	*muttajji* 'great grandmother'
G^{+2}	*taata* 'grandfather'	*ammaNNi* 'grandmother'
		ajji 'grandmother'
G^{+1}	*tande* 'father'	*taayi* 'mother'
	appa 'father'	*amma* 'mother'
	doDDappa 'father's elder brother'	*doDDamma* 'mother's elder sister'
	cikkappa 'father's younger brother'	*cikkamma* 'mother's younger sister'
$G^{=}$	*aNNa* 'elder brother'	*akka* 'elder sister'
	tamma 'younger brother'	*taŋgi* 'younger sister'
G^{-1}	*maga* 'son'	*magaLu* 'daughter'
G^{-2}	*momaga* 'grandson'	*momagaLu* 'granddaughter'
G^{-3}	*mumaga* 'great grandson'	*mumagaLu* 'great granddaughter'

Componential Definitions of the Primary Senses

The primary senses of the terms may be defined by a feature of root meaning (K *sambanda* 'relation') and five dimensions of contrast: generation ($G^{\leq 3}$), relative age in generation ($\pm$), sex of propositus (δ_p, $♀_p$), and sex of alter (δ, $♀$), and linkage (see below, and appendix 1 for complete list of notations).

The dimension 'linkage' is composed of two logically distinct factors, one of collaterality distinguishing lineal, colineal, and several degrees of collaterality, and one of relative sex distinguishing links traced through same-sex (parallel) or opposite-sex (cross) siblings or cousins. Of course the factor of relative sex-links applies only to collateral kinsmen. By the combination of these two factors the focal senses of the terms contrast according to six features: L (lineal), Co-L (colineal), $//Co^1$ (first degree parallel collateral), XCo^1 (first degree cross-collateral), and XCo^2 (second degree cross-collateral).

These semantic dimensions do not play equivalent roles in the definitions of the terms. For one thing, two of the five dimensions, sex of ego and sex of alter, are not, strictly speaking, genealogical. That is, they are properties of categories of designated relatives, not of the genealogical connection between them. In addition, of the five dimensions, linkage is the most complex and most important in accounting for the extension of terms to distant kintypes. Further, since the terminology is not a perfect paradigm, not all dimensions of contrast are represented in the significata of each term.

The componential definitions of the primary senses, represented as semantic features in the five dimensions of contrast, are given in table 4.1. The first dimension of contrast, generation, is realized in the definition of every term in the corpus as one of seven generations (from third ascending to third descending). The second dimension, relative age in generation, is contrastive for all focal senses in the generation of the propositus. It is also contrastive among the parallel collaterals of parents' generation who are older or younger than the linking parent of the propositus. The fourth dimension, sex of alter, is realized in every definition; the fifth, sex of propositus, is realized in only two definitions, that of *maida* 'woman's younger male cross-cousin' and that of *baamaida* 'man's younger male cross-cousin'.

The third dimension, type of linkage, is the most complex and the most interesting. It is through the neutralizations of contrasting types of linkages that terms are extended beyond their focal kintypes. The assignment of more distant collaterals to the cross and parallel categories, the merging of lineal and parallel collaterals, and the merging of in-laws with cross-collaterals typify this as a Dravidian system of kin classification. The rules which account for these extensions are presented in the next section.

The Extension Rules

Rules may be written to specify the ways in which kinship terms are extended from their focal denotata to more distant denotata. Having determined the foci of each term and noted how the focal senses may be defined componentially, we may now consider the full range of denotata for each term in order to arrive at the set of rules which will relate these denotata to the focal kintypes. The relationship is shown by a set of rules which reduce the more distant denotata to the focal kintype of each term, thereby showing (in reverse) the derivations that distribute terms to kintypes in the genealogical network. Appendix 2 is a list of kin terms with focal and more distant denotata, giving the rules by which terms are extended to each of the denotata.

Seven rules and their corollaries are sufficient. The first three are of wide distribution in systems of kin classification; the fourth, fifth, and sixth are specifically Dravidian and account for the distribution of terms to distant collaterals and the merging of in-laws with cross-collaterals. The seventh rule is structurally auxilliary; it gives alternate designations for some kintypes that are the result of the preference for marriages between mother's younger brother and elder sister's daughter.

Rule 1. The Half-Sibling Rule. According to this rule a child of one's parent is structurally equivalent to one's sibling (FS→B; FD→Z; MS→B; MD→Z).

In Kannada, as in most other systems of kin classification, half-siblings are terminologically equated with full siblings and classified terminologically as *aNNa* B+, *akka* Z+, *tamma* B−, and *taŋgi* Z−.

Rule 2. The Stepkin Rule. According to this rule a parent's spouse (stepmother or stepfather) is structurally equivalent to a parent and, reciprocally, a spouse's child (stepchild) is structurally equivalent to one's own child (FW→M, reciprocally HC→C; and MH→F, reciprocally WC→C).

Like rule 1, this rule occurs in a great many systems of kin classification. In Kannada it means that stepparents belong terminologically to the parent class and are designated by the same terms as parents (*amma* M, *appa* F) or by the terms for the subclasses of the parent class (e.g., FW younger than real M may be called *cikkamma* MZ−). Reciprocally, stepchildren are terminologically equated with one's own children (*maga* S, and *magaLu* D).

Rule 3. The Same-Sex Sibling Merging Rule. According to this rule, a person's sibling of the same sex is structurally equivalent to that person him/herself as a link to a more distant kinsman.

$$(\male B \ldots \to \male \ldots) \equiv (\ldots \male B \to \ldots \male)$$
$$(\female Z \ldots \to \female \ldots) \equiv (\ldots \female Z \to \ldots \female).$$

Thus, for example, in Kannada a man's brother is structurally equivalent to himself as a link to a more distant relative; therefore, a man's brother's child is terminologically equivalent to a man's own child (both are *maga* S or *magaLu* D). Similarly, a woman's sister, as a link, is equivalent to a woman herself; thus, a woman's sister's child is terminologically the same as a woman's own child (again *maga* S or *magaLu* D).

Beginning with the next rule, rule 4, we encounter those structural equivalences that are characteristic of Dravidian systems of kin classification. The fourth rule, together with the first three, account for the extension of kinship terms to more distant collaterals by specifying the ways in which cross-cousins serve as links to more distant kinsmen.

Rule 4. The Cross/Parallel Generalization Rule. According to this rule one's father's cross-cousin is structurally equivalent to one's mother's sibling, and, reciprocally, one's male cross-cousin's $(PSb_x S)$ child is equivalent to one's sister's child. Similarly, one's mother's cross-cousin is structurally equivalent to one's father's sibling, and, reciprocally, one's female cross-cousin's child is structurally equivalent to one's brother's child:

$$(FPSb_x C \rightarrow MSb) \equiv (PSb_x SC \rightarrow ZC)$$
$$(MPSb_x C \rightarrow FSb) \equiv (PSb_x DC \rightarrow BC)$$

Thus,

$$(FMBD \rightarrow MZ) \equiv (♀FZSC \rightarrow ♀ZC)$$
$$(FFZD \rightarrow MZ) \equiv (♀MBSC \rightarrow ♀ZC)$$
$$(FMBS \rightarrow MB) \equiv (♂FZSC \rightarrow ♂ZC)$$
$$(FFZS \rightarrow MB) \equiv (♂MBSC \rightarrow ♂ZC)$$

and,

$$(MMBD \rightarrow FZ) \equiv (♀FZDC \rightarrow ♀BC)$$
$$(MFZD \rightarrow FZ) \equiv (♀MBDC \rightarrow ♀BC)$$
$$(MMBS \rightarrow FB) \equiv (♂FZDC \rightarrow ♂BC)$$
$$(MFZS \rightarrow FB) \equiv (♂MBDC \rightarrow ♂BC).$$

The import of this rule is that the sum of two cross-links is a parallel link (i.e., the children of opposite-sex cross-cousins are 'siblings'), while the sum of a parallel link and a cross-link (or a cross-link and a parallel link) is a cross-link (i.e., the children of same-sex cross-cousins are 'cross-cousins'). The other possibility, the sum of two parallel links, is taken care of by the same-sex sibling merging rule and the half-sibling rule so that, for example, a man's father's brother's son is equivalent to a man's father's son (by the same-sex sibling merging rule), and a man's father's son is equivalent to a man's brother (by the half-sibling rule).

Rule 5. The Cross/Parallel Neutralization Rule. This rule neutralizes the cross/parallel contrast for designated kinsmen of the second and third ascending and descending generations. Thus, one's opposite-sex siblings' child's child is terminologically equivalent to one's same-sex sibling's child's child. Reciprocally, a parent's parent's opposite-sex sibling is structurally equivalent to a parent's parent's same-sex sibling as designated relative. Thus,

$$(.Sb_x CC \rightarrow .Sb_{//} CC) \equiv (PPSb_x. \rightarrow PPSb_{//}.).$$

This rule is written at the level of the grandparent/grandchild super-classes in which sex of alter is not distinguished. When the rule is applied, the equivalences it sets up must conform to the sex of ego and the designated kinsman. Thus,

$$(.ZCC \rightarrow .BCC) \equiv (PMB. \rightarrow PFB.)$$
$$(.BCC \rightarrow .ZCC) \equiv (PFZ. \rightarrow PMZ.).$$

Since rules 4 and 5 may appear to be complicated (but are not, as we shall see below), a few examples are given to show how these rules are applied in combination with the first three rules to reduce distant denotata to focal kintypes.

Example 1. FFZSD+, terminologically *attige* 'elder female cross-cousin'. Scanning rules 1 through 5 we see that the only rule applicable is rule 4: FFZS is equivalent to MB, and his daughter (MBD) is by definition a cross-cousin of the propositus. Because she is older (+) than the propositus, she is $PSb_x D+$, *attige*.

Example 2. ♂FZDD, terminologically *magaLu* 'daughter'. Here, rule 4 again applies: a man's parent's opposite-sex sibling's daughter's child (in general, $PSb_x DC$, and in this case ♂FZDD) is equivalent to that man's brother's child. Therefore, ♂FZDD→♂BD. And, since by rule 3, the same-sex sibling merging rule, a man's brother as a link is equivalent to that man as a link (♂B ... →♂ ...), the expression is further reduced to ♂D or *magaLu* by definition.

Example 3. ♂FFMBS, terminologically *taata* 'grandfather'. By rule 4 father's same-sex cross-cousin is equivalent to mother's brother (FMBS→MB). Therefore, the expression ♂FFMBS is reduced to ♂FMB. By rule 5, the cross/parallel neutralization rule, a parent's parent's opposite-sex sibling is equivalent to a parent's parent's same-sex sibling. Therefore, a man's father's mother's brother

(δFMB) is equivalent to his father's father (δFF), who is *taata* 'grandfather' by definition.

The sixth rule accounts for the terminological equivalence of certain in-laws with certain consanguineal relatives.

Rule 6. The In-Law Merging Rule. According to this rule, a spouse's parent is structurally equivalent to parent's opposite-sex sibling: and reciprocally, a child's spouse is structurally equivalent to one's opposite-sex sibling's child:

$$(SpP \rightarrow PSb_x) \equiv (CSp \rightarrow Sb_xC),$$

that is,

$$(WF \rightarrow MB) \equiv (\delta DH \rightarrow \delta ZS)$$
$$(HF \rightarrow MB) \equiv (\delta SW \rightarrow \delta ZD)$$
$$(WM \rightarrow FZ) \equiv (\female DH \rightarrow \female BS)$$
$$(HM \rightarrow FZ) \equiv (\female SW \rightarrow \female BD).$$

A corollary of this rule is that one's spouse's sibling is structurally equivalent to a cross-cousin and, reciprocally, one's sibling's spouse is structurally equivalent to a cross-cousin.
Thus,

$$(SpSb \rightarrow PSb_xC) \equiv (SbSp \rightarrow PSb_xC),$$

that is,

$$(HB \rightarrow MBS/FZS) \equiv (\delta BW \rightarrow FZD/MBD)$$
$$(HZ \rightarrow MBD/FZD) \equiv (\female BW \rightarrow MBD/FZD)$$
$$(WB \rightarrow MBS/FZS) \equiv (\delta ZH \rightarrow MBS/FZS)$$
$$(WZ \rightarrow MBD/FZD) \equiv (\female ZH \rightarrow MBS/FZS).$$

Another important corollary of this rule is that a parent's opposite-sex sibling's child's spouse is equivalent to a sibling and, reciprocally, a spouse's parent's opposite-sex sibling's child is equivalent to a sibling:

$$(PSb_xCSp \rightarrow Sb) \equiv (SpPSb_xC \rightarrow Sb).$$

This sixth rule, along with the other four, will reduce all distant relatives to the focal members of the kin classes to which they belong. There are, as a residue, some alternate usages that may be accounted for in a seventh rule. However, before turning to it, it would be perhaps helpful to give a few examples of the application of the six rules.

Example 4. HFBS+, terminologically *baava* MBS+/FZS+. There are two orders in which the rules can be applied, but the result is the

same. Applying rule 6, the in-law merging rule, HF is equivalent to
MB giving MBBS+. Applying rule 3, the same-sex sibling merging
rule (a corollary of which would state that MBB→MB), the expression is reduced to MBS+, *baava* by definition. By another route,
rule 3, the same-sex sibling merging rule (FB→B), is first applied,
and the expression is reduced to HFS+. By applying rule 6, the
in-law merging rule (HF→MB), the expression is again reduced to
MBS+. Thus by both routes application of the rules reduces the
expression to MBS+ which is *baava* by definition.

Example 5. MZHBSW+, terminologically *attige* MBD+/FZD+. By
rule 3, the same-sex sibling merging rule, MZ→M, and the expression is reduced to MHBSW+. By rule 2, the step kin rule, MH→F,
and the expression is reduced to FBSW+. By rule 3, the same-sex
sibling merging rule, FB→F, and the expression is further reduced
to FSW+. By rule 1, the half-sibling merging rule, FS→B, and the
expression is reduced to BW+. By rule 6, the in-law equation rule,
BW+ is finally reduced to MBD+/FZD+, which is *attige* by definition.

In appendix 2, the lists of denotata, some kin types occur under two
kin terms. One of these usages is accounted for by the set of six equivalence rules. This is its principal designation. The other usage is an
alternative that is not accounted for by the equivalence rules given thus
far and may be accounted for by an auxilliary rule to be posited below.
In the lists of denotata accompanying each term, the alternative denotata
are separated from the principal denotata by a dotted line. In every case
the alternative denotata are of a different genealogical generation from
the principal denotata of the term. This merging of generations can be
understood in the context of the preference for intergenerational
mother's younger brother-elder sister's daughter marriage. Such alternative designations are not necessarily the product of an actual uncle-niece
marriage, but may be applied when the age of the designated kinsman is
closer to a generation other than the genealogical generation. These
alternative designations are accounted for in rule 7.

Rule 7. The Uncle-Niece Marriage In-law Merging Rule. According
to this rule, a woman's husband's parent is equivalent to a woman's
mother's parent and, reciprocally, one's son's wife is equivalent to
one's daughter's daughter:
$$(♀HP→♀MP) \equiv (SW→DD).$$

In addition, a man's wife's mother is equivalent to a man's elder sister and, reciprocally, a woman's daughter's husband is equivalent to a woman's younger brother:

$$(\male WM \rightarrow \male Z+) \equiv (\female DH \rightarrow \female B-).$$

A corollary of this rule is that a man's wife's father is equivalent to the man's elder sister's husband and, reciprocally, a man's daughter's husband is equivalent to his wife's younger brother:

$$(\male WF \rightarrow \male Z+H) \equiv (\male DH \rightarrow \male WB-).$$

A further corollary of this rule accounts for the children of spouse's parents, that is, spouse's siblings. A woman's husband's sibling is equivalent to a woman's mother's sibling and, reciprocally, one's brother's wife is equivalent to one's sister's daughter:

$$(\female HSb \rightarrow \female MSb) \equiv (BW \rightarrow ZD).$$

Similarly, a man's wife's sibling is equivalent to a man's elder sister's child and, reciprocally, one's sister's husband is equivalent to one's mother's younger brother:

$$(\male WSb \rightarrow \male Z+C) \equiv (ZH \rightarrow MB-).$$

It is difficult to say under what conditions rule 7 takes precedence over rule 6, the in-law merging rule. There are two cases when it almost always does so, husband's elder sister and elder male cross-cousin. A woman's husband's elder sister, who by rules 1 to 6 (and according to many male informants) is *attige* FZD+/MBD+, is consistently referred to as *cikkamma* MZ− even when she is not a mother's younger sister (which could happen if the woman had married her mother's classificatory brother). Thus, according to the corollary of rule 7, $\female$HZ+$\rightarrow \female$MZ− or *cikkamma*. It seems to be important that this term signifies a senior generation and is therefore more deferential than *attige* FZD+/MBD+.

The other kinsman consistently called in a fashion that results from the application of this auxilliary rule is elder male cross-cousin, real and classificatory, terminologically *baava*. Indeed, the expression *baava* is seldom used in the village, *maava* MB usually being substituted for it. This usage is very tentatively accounted for in the following way. An equivalence between elder male cross-cousin and mother's brother is created by the coexistence of rule 6, the in-law merging rule, in which husband's elder brother is equivalent to a woman's elder male cross-cousin ($\female$HB+$\rightarrow \female$PSb$_x$S+), and rule 7, the uncle-niece in-law merging rule, in which husband's elder brother is equivalent to mother's younger brother ($♀HB→MB-$). Thus, since two things equivalent to the same thing are equivalent to each other:

($♀HB+→♀PSb_xS+$)
and ($♀HB+→♀MB-$)
∴ ($♀PSb_xS+↔♀MB-$).

Similarly, by rule 6 a man's wife's father is equivalent to his mother's brother ($♂WF→MB$), but by a corollary of rule 7 a man's wife's father is equivalent to his elder sister's husband ($♂WF→♂Z+H$), who (by rule 6) is equivalent to an elder male cross-cousin ($♂ZH→PSb_xS$). Thus a man's elder male cross-cousin is equivalent to his mother's brother:

($♂WF→♂MB$)
and ($♂WF→♂Z+H→♂PSb_xS+$)
∴ ($♂MB ↔ ♂PSb_xS+$).

As with the use of *cikkamma* MZ− to designate husband's elder sister, the use of *maava* MB to designate elder male cross-cousins is apparently preferred because it is close and more deferential: *maava* MB signifies a senior generation, and a closer relationship to ego—first degree collateral rather than second degree collateral. Thus these two usages signify greater deference and closeness. In addition to these consistent usages, other usages also accounted for by rule 7 tend to occur when rule 7 equivalences place the designated relative in a generational category more appropriate to his or her age.

Because this rule is not consistently applied and because it results in alternative designations for certain kin types, it is auxilliary to the basic semantic system of kin classification. Its peculiar status is also evident in its application, which is apparently often in violation of the principle of consistency of reciprocals. That is, the reciprocal of *maava* MB is *aLiya* $♂$ZS, $♀$BS, but when an elder male cross-cousin is referred to as *maava,* the younger male cross-cousin may still be *baamaida* PSb_xC, not *aLiya* $♂$ZS, $♀$BS. Similarly, the reciprocal of *cikkamma* MZ− is *magaLu* D or *maga* S, but if a woman refers to her husband's elder sister as *cikkamma* MZ−, she is nevertheless *naadini* B−W, PSb_xD− to her husband's elder sister.

With these six basic rules and the one auxilliary rule, all of the denotata in appendix 2 can be reduced to the focal kin type of the kin class to which they belong. Appendix 2 shows, next to each denotatum, the rules which need to be employed in that reduction. These rules account for the relations among the multiple denotata of each kinship term. Having accounted for the relationships between the members of each kin class, it is possible to offer definitions for each class as a whole. Elements in these definitions are established by the neutralizations proposed in the rules discussed in this section. Thus the expansion rules are necessary not only for understanding the relationships among denotata of the terms, but for the definition of the kin classes themselves.

Expanded Kin-Class Definitions

In the first section of this chapter componential definitions of the focal senses of each kin term were posited using five semantic dimensions: (1) generation of designated relative ($G^{\leq 3}$); (2) relative age within generation of designated relative ($\pm$); (3) type of linkage (L, Co-L, $//Co^1$, XCo^1, XCo^2); (4) sex of alter (δ, $\female$); (5) sex of propositus (δ_p, $\female_p$). Of these dimensions, three are expressed in the same way in each denotatum of a given term: (2) relative age within generation is always either older or younger for all denotata of a term whose focal type is either older or younger than the propositus or the linking parent of the propositus; (4) sex of alter is either male or female for all the denotata of a term; (5) sex of propositus, contrastive only for two terms in the corpus, is always male for *baamaida* 'man's younger male cross-cousin etc.' and female for *maida* 'woman's younger-male cross cousin, younger sister's husband etc.'. The first dimension of contrast, generation, is a bit more complex. At the end of the lists of denotata of each term are kin types that are not of the same generation as the focal denotatum. These are, as has been shown, alternative usages and not a part of the basic structure of the system of kin classification. The extension of terms to these denotata was accounted for by an auxilliary rule arising from the preference for uncle-niece marriage. Because these uses and the rule that accounts for them go beyond the basic structure of the system of kin classification, they are excluded from componential definitions of the kin classes. With the denotata accounted for by rule 7 eliminated, the remaining denotata of each term are of one genealogical generation.

Thus the semantic features of the focal senses from the dimensions (1) generation, (2) relative age in generation, (4) sex of designated relative, and (5) sex of propositus are also among the defining features of the class of relatives designated by that term. The last dimension, the type of linkage, is more complicated.

The features of this dimension represented in the focal senses of the terms are lineal, colineal, first and second degrees cross-collateral, and first degree parallel collateral. The additional denotata included more distant cross- and parallel-collaterals and relatives related through marriage. The expansion rules in the previous section, which give the relationship among multiple denotata of a term, show how the five types of linkage distinctive in the definitions of the focal kin classes are combined, and occur, in the total kin class definitions, as a binary opposition between 'noncross' and 'cross' linkage. Expanded kin

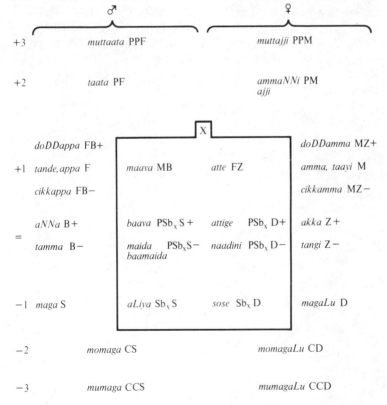

Figure 4.1   **Semantic Structure of Expanded Kin Classes**

classes contain either cross-collaterals and in-laws, or lineals, colineals, and parallel collaterals. Thus, the definition of each kin class contains either the feature 'cross' (X) or the feature 'noncross' ($\overline{\text{X}}$). The cross-parallel neutralization rule for the second and third ascending and descending generations (rule 5) results in 'noncross' terms being applied to all relatives of those generations. Thus when the opposition between 'cross' and 'noncross' kin classes is neutralized, terms for 'noncross' classes appear, indicating that in the opposition between 'cross' and 'noncross' kin categories, terms defined with the feature 'cross' are the marked, and those with the feature 'noncross' the unmarked, members of the opposition.

Table 4.1 includes the definitions of the expanded kin classes according to the five semantic dimensions. Figure 4.1 is a diagrammatic presentation of the semantic structure of the kin classes so defined. The expansion rules, giving the relationships among the multiple denotata of the terms, and the definitions of the expanded kin classes summarize the semantic structure of the Kannada system of kin classification and provide the basis for considering the occurrence and meaning of kin terms in address.

5 Kinship Terms of Address

Vocative and Referential Terminologies

The anthropological literature on kinship is abundant with analyses of terms of reference, but contains little on terms for address. This situation exists despite the fact that ethnographers customarily distinguish and report both vocative and referential terminologies. The general lack of attention to kinship terms of address is not difficult to account for. The following remarks from Murdock are characteristic of a widely accepted approach to kinship terms for address:

> Some peoples have completely distinct sets of terms for address and reference, others make only grammatical distinctions or none at all, and still others have varying combinations.
>
> Terms of reference are normally more specific in their application than terms of address.... Moreover terms of reference are usually more complete than terms of address.
>
> It may be customary to use only personal names in addressing certain relatives. Furthermore terms of address tend to reveal more duplication and overlapping than do terms of reference. For these reasons, terms of reference are much more useful in kinship analysis, and are consequently used exclusively in the present work. [Murdock 1949, p. 98]

This statement describes the differences between terms of address and terms of reference. It maintains that there are two distinguishable systems which may have some, all, or no terms in common. Because terminologies of address are less complete (one infers that 'complete' refers to the partitioning of the universe of kinsmen); because terms of address often are used to a wider array of kinsmen and even to nonkin and therefore overlap as alternate designations for the same relative; and because other terms, such as personal names, are often substituted for kinship terms in address, Murdock concludes that terms of reference are better for kinship analysis, that is, the discovery of lexically labeled classes of kinsmen. His observations are widely applicable and certainly fit the situation reported here for Kannada. But the question remaining unanswered by this descriptive account of terms for address is what basically is the difference between address and reference? For Murdock the answer is as follows:

> A term of address is one used in speaking to a relative; it is part of the linguistic behavior characteristic of the particular interpersonal relationship. A term of reference is one used to designate a relative in speaking about him to a third person; it is thus not part of the relationship itself, but a word denoting a person who occupies a particular kinship status. [Murdock 1949, p. 97]

His meaning here is not entirely clear. The first half of each statement simply says that address terms are used in address (to a second person), while reference terms are used to refer (about a third person). The second half of each statement is both more important and more obscure. The use of a term of address is part of a social interaction (between speaker and addressee) while the use of a term of reference is not, since it refers to a genealogical relation involving someone who is not participating in the speech act. Murdock appreciated that terms of address are somehow inextricably tied to social interaction and that this distinguishes them from terms of reference, although he did not attempt to develop the implications of this view.

Perhaps the only analysis of a system of kinship terms of address is Conant's 1961 paper on Jarawa kinship terminology. Conant was motivated to do the analysis because he observed, contrary to the generalization made by Murdock, that terms of address in Jarawa provide more complete information about kin classification than do terms of reference. However, Conant's analysis appears a bit strange. He felt compelled to include terms not normally considered kinship terms because they are used in address to classes of kinsmen. Conant's discomfort with this result (p. 31) led him to inquire about the distinction between address and reference: "Or is the difference between systems of address and reference much less, perhaps only a situational difference involving different frames of reference?" His query about 'situational differences' and 'frames of reference' is not developed and therefore is difficult to interpret. His remark exemplifies both the common recognition that there is a difference between terms of reference and terms of address, and the lack of clarity about just what the difference is.

In contrast, Schneider (1969, 1970) questioned the very basis of the distinction between reference and address in the analysis of American kinship terminology: "and even if it were possible to show two distinct systems of terminology and even if the distinction could be applied to American kinship terms, there remain no valid practical or theoretical grounds for such exclusions" of terms of address in an analysis of kinship terminology (1969, p. 23). For him, then, the distinction between address and reference systems is of doubtful significance theoretically and practically and only obscures real problems by allowing certain terms to be excluded from analysis on the grounds that they are terms of address, thus, according to Schneider, artificially simplifying the corpus by avoiding the realities of alternate and overlapping terms.

There are, however, very solid demonstrable theoretical and practical grounds for distinguishing two systems of terms for classifying kinsmen. Furthermore, there is a sound basis for "the assumption that somehow the referential system is closer to the classification of kinsmen, the content of the kin categories, or the ways in which the semantic space occupied by kintypes is partitioned" (Schneider 1968, p. 89). Here Murdock's observation that terms for address are part and parcel of social interaction, while terms of reference are not, is crucial.

The major obstacle to an understanding of terms for address is the view current in linguistics and ethnographic semantics that semantics is the study of symbolic meaning alone. That is, that the meaning of a term, its significations literal or figurative, and its connotations are all specifiable solely in terms of symbolic meaning.

Even if terms of address refer to the same category of kinsmen (that is, have the same symbolic meaning) as kinship terms of reference, the total definition is different. Kinship terms of reference are wholly symbolic signs; they signify attributes of the class of kin types they designate. Kinship terms of address are in part symbolic and in part indexical signs: in addition to referring to a class of kin types, they indicate the addressee, actually calling to his attention that the utterance is directed at him. Thus an indexical component of meaning, 'existentially associated with the addressee', is part of the definition. This indexical component does not refer to an attribute of its object, but indicates its object by its connection to it. This is the relation between address and interaction that Murdock hazily perceived: in part, the sense of a sign functioning indexically is its connection to its users. The presence of nonsymbolic meaning in terms for address provides a valid theoretical and practical basis for distinguishing address and reference and is therefore an answer to Schneider's skepticism. In this chapter kinship terms of address are considered as indexical symbols related both to other kinship terms in the system of kin classification (analyzed in chapter 4) and to other second person indexes in the system of address.

The Corpus

Terms for address in Kannada usually occur at the beginning or end of an utterance, and are often marked by case affixes and/or by intonation. The vocative intonation contour is rising in contrast with the slightly falling nonvocative intonation. In conjunction with the rising intonation, the final vowel of the stem is sometimes lengthened and louder. In addition there are three vocative suffixes: *-oo* 'vocative' (e.g., *ammoo*); *-lee* 'vocative masculine' (e.g., *appalee* 'father, voc.'); *-gee* 'vocative feminine', used only by members of the A.K. jaati (e.g., *ammagee* 'mother, voc.'); and one prefix *d-* occurring only with *amma* 'mother' (*damma*).

Table 5.1 is a list of the kinship terms used in address. Each is given with the focal kintype (which is, in every case except *tande* 'father' and *taayi* 'mother', the same in reference and address) and with the componential definition of the extended class of kinsmen designated by the term as established in the preceding chapter.

In comparison with the corpus of kin terms used to refer to genealogical relationships, this corpus is limited in some ways and expanded in others. The corpus includes only those terms whose foci are senior to the propositus and whose componential definitions contain a feature of ascending generation or seniority within ego's generation ($G^{=}. +$). The reciprocals of these terms, whose definitions contain a feature of juniority and/or descending generation, do not occur in address. Persons belonging to junior categories may be addressed by name. Three terms

Table 5.1 **Kin Terms for Address**

taata	PF	$K.G^{+2}.\male$
ajji *ammaNNi*	PM	$K.G^{+2}.\female$
tande	(F)	
appa	F	$K.L.G^{+1}.\male$
doDDappa	FB+	$K.\bar{X}.G^{+1}.+.\male$
cikkappa *ciccappa* *appappa*	FB−	$K.\bar{X}.G^{+1}.\male$
taayi	(M)	
amma	M	$K.L.G^{+1}.\female$
doDDamma	MZ+	$K.\bar{X}.G^{+1}.+.\female$
cikkamma *ciccamma* *cicci*	MZ−	$K.\bar{X}.G^{+1}.-.\female$
atte	FZ	$K.X.G^{+1}.\female$
maava *maama*	MB	$K.X.G^{+1}.\male$
attige	PSb$_x$D+	$K.X.G^{-}.+.\female$
aNNa	B+	$K.\bar{X}.G^{-}.+.\male$
akka	Z+	$K.\bar{X}.G^{-}.+.\female$

for senior kinsmen do not occur in this corpus: the great grandparent terms, *muttaata* PPF and *muttajji* PPM, and the term for senior male cross-cousin, *baava* PSb$_x$S+.

The address reciprocal (kin term for senior, name for junior) provides further evidence that the kinship terms for address are part of a semantic domain partitioned by all terms of address. All senior kinsmen are opposed to all junior kinsmen. The former are addressed with kinship terms differentiated by kin status, the latter by personal name. Thus one set of reciprocals has the symbolic components 'Kinship' and 'Senior relative age' or 'Generation ascending' in common, while the other set has no common symbolic components. Both, however, have the common indexical component, the root feature of the domain of address, 'existentially associated with the addressee'.

In Kannada reciprocal kin statuses are almost always asymmetrical (not self-reciprocal),[1] and one status is senior to the other. Therefore the use of a kin term in address to a kinsman indicates an asymmetrical relationship in which the speaker is subordinate and expects to receive a personal name in return. The use of a kinship term in address, by signifying the addressee's status as a senior kinsman, is a way of expressing deference toward or respect for him.

Another notable feature of the corpus is the number of alternate sets of terms:

1. *ammaNNi*   PM
   ajji
2. *tande*   F
   appa
3. *amma*   M
   taayi
4. *maava*   MB
   maama
5. *cikkappa*   FB−
   ciccappa
   appappa
6. *cikkamma*   MZ−
   ciccamma
   cicci

The first three pairs are terms not formally related to one another. In the corpus of terms for classifying kinsmen, the pairs are synonymous. However, in address they are used differently: members of the A.K. caste use *ajji* PM more often than *ammaNNi* PM; *tande* and *taayi* do not occur in address to kinsmen. The basis of these different usages is discussed when the metaphorical senses of terms are analyzed in a later section of this chapter.

The remaining three sets contain terms that are formally similar, in which the second and third forms are phonological simplifications of the first and do not occur in the corpus of terms for classifying kinsmen. These are related to the first listed form as phonological simplifications by the assimilation of the second consonant to the first: *maava* →*maama, cikkappa→ciccappa,* and *cikkamma→ciccamma.* While formally *maama* appears to be a simplified version of *maava,* etymologically *maama* is a borrowing from Sanskrit, taking the form *maava* in Kannada (Kittle 1894). *Appappa* is derived by the reduplication of the term for the focus (*appa* 'father') of the superclass to which father's younger brother belongs. *Cicci* is derived from *ciccamma* by dropping *amma* and subsistuting for it the feminine suffix -*i.*

Cikkamma MZ— and *cikkappa* FB— are rare as terms for address; *ciccamma* MZ— and *ciccappa* FB— are common; *appappa* FB— and *cicci MZ* — are primarily used by children. *Maava* MB occurs only rarely in address, *maama* MB being the more usual form. These pairs of terms are distinct sociolinguistically, not semantically; that is, their pattern of use is distinguishable, but their pragmatic and symbolic definitions are the same.

The Occurrence of Kin Terms
in Address to Kinsmen

In this section the occurrence of each of these terms in address is described, beginning with terms designating second ascending generation kin classes. Each term is given with its focal kin type as a gloss. Then its occurrence in address to kinsmen is compared with its occurrence in referring to kinship statuses.

taata PF may be used in address to any male kinsman of the second or higher ascending generations. However, in address to focal members of the class FF and MF, *appa* F often replaces *taata*.

ajji and *ammaNNi* PM may be used to address any female kinsman of the second or higher ascending generation, the latter term occurring more frequently in the speech of the higher castes. In address to the focal members of the class (FM and MM), *amma* M often replaces *ajji* PM and *ammaNNi* PM.

tande F and *taayi* M are not used to address father, mother, or other kinsmen. Their metaphoric use in address to nonkin is taken up in a later section.

appa F is used commonly to address the following kinsmen: F, FB+, PF, HF. In address, therefore, it overlaps with *doDDappa* FB+, *taata* PF, and *maama* HF.

amma M is used to address the following kinsmen: M, MZ+, FB+W, PM, HM, and therefore in address overlaps with *doDDamma* MZ+, FB+W, *ajji/ammaNNi* PM, and *atte* HM.

doDDappa FB+ is used to address the same kinsmen for whom it is used in reference. That is, it is used to FB+ and by extension to the class K.$\overline{\text{X}}$.G^{+1}.+.♂. As a term of address, however, it is restricted since many people prefer to use *appa* F to address the focus of the class FB+.

doDDamma MZ+ is used in address as it is used in reference, to

MZ+ and by extension to the class K.$\overline{\text{X}}$.G^{+1}.+.♀. Like *doDDappa* FB+, its occurrence is restricted by the common use of *amma* M in address to MZ+ and FBW+.

cikkamma MZ− and its two formal variants *ciccamma* and *cicci* occur in address to the same persons for whom *cikkamma* is used in reference: MZ−, the widened class K.$\overline{\text{X}}$.G^{+1}.−.♀, and by the special uncle-niece marriage extension rule HZ+. *Akka* Z+ is sometimes substituted for these forms in address.

cikkappa FB− and its formal variants *ciccappa* and *appappa* are used in address to FB− and members of the widened class K.$\overline{\text{X}}$.G^{+1}.−.♂. *aNNa* B+ is sometimes substituted for these forms in address.

maava MB and its variant *maama* MB are used to address MB, the members of the widened class K.X.G^{+1}.♂, and senior male cross-cousins. Occasionally *maama* occurs in address to younger male classificatory cross-cousins, if their names are not known. Its occurrence is limited because many women address HF as *appa* F rather than *maama,* and elder male cross-cousins are often addressed as *aNNa* B+ (or name with *aNNa*).

attige PSb$_x$D+ occurs in address to the same kinsmen for whom it is used in reference: elder female cross-cousins and the expanded class K.X.G$^{..}$.+.♀. It occurrence in address is limited by a reluctance to use the term which is sometimes replaced by *akka* Z+ or simply dropped so that no kinship term is used in address.

aNNa B+ is used to address the same kinsmen for whom it is used in reference, B+, and the expanded class K.$\overline{\text{X}}$.G$^{..}$.+.♂. In addition it often replaces *maama* MB in address to Z+H, MB, FZS+, MBS+, and *cikkappa* FB− in address to real or classificatory FB−, and occasionally even *doDDappa* FB+ in address to real or classificatory FB+. *aNNa* is especially common in address to more distant elder male classificatory kinsmen, who might come from other villages to a wedding or funeral.

akka Z+ occurs in address to the same women for whom it is used in reference: Z+ and the extended class K.$\overline{\text{X}}$.G$^{..}$.+.♀. In addition it is used to address some women referred to as *cikkamma* MZ−, especially FBW− and HZ+; *atte* FZ, only WM and FZ−; and *attige* classificatory elder female cross-cousins.

Figure 5.1 gives the possible address forms for focal kintypes, showing the alternate forms for each.

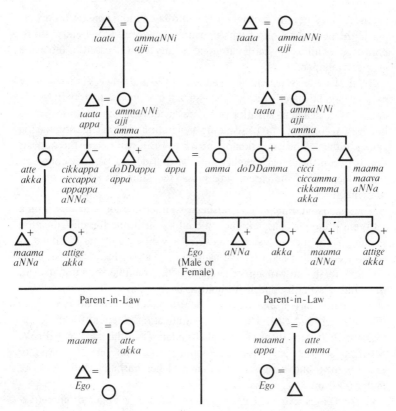

Figure 5.1   **Possible Address Forms for Focal Kin Types**

The Definitions of Kin Terms of Address

Some of the kinship terms used in address are extended to denotata not
included in the referential designatum of the term. The designata of
some terms remain the same in address as in reference: *doDDappa*
FB+, *doDDamma* MZ+, *cikkappa* FB−, *cikkamma* MZ−, *atte* FZ,
and *attige* PSb$_x$D+. Terms whose designata are expanded in address are
ajji PM, *ammaNNi* PM, *taata* PF, *appa* F, *amma* M, *maama* MB, *aNNa*
B+, and *akka* Z+.

The grandparent terms (*taata* PF, *ajji* PM, and *ammaNNi* PM) are all extended in address to kinsmen in the third ascending generation resulting in the neutralization of the opposition between second and third or higher generations so that great grandparents are addressed in the same way as grandparents.

Appa 'father' is extended in address to grandfather, father's elder brother, and husband's father. The extension of *appa* F to grandfather is again based on a neutralization of contrasts between generations, that is, between second and first ascending generation, so that grandfather is called 'father'. The extension of *appa* F to FB+ neutralizes the opposition between the lineal member and the first degree parallel collateral senior member of the parent superclass (see same-sex sibling merging rule chapter 4).

The extension of *appa* F to husband's father in address is based on a different principle, one not encountered so far in the kin classification system. Here the opposition between a woman and her husband is neutralized so that she uses the same term that he does. This usage is probably related to women's change in family membership at marriage, from father's family and household to husband's.

The extensions of *amma* M in address parallel those of *appa* F: to FB+W, PM, and HM. The same neutralizations account for these extensions: between lineal and parallel collateral in the case of FB+W, between second and first ascending generation in the case of grandmother, and between a woman and her husband in the case of mother-in-law.

aNNa B+ is extended in address to father's younger brother (*cikkappa*), sister's husband older than ego (*baava*), and senior real and classificatory male cross-cousins (*baava*). The extension to father's younger brother is based on the neutralization of the contrast between elders in own generation ($G^{=}.+$) and juniors in the parental generation ($G^{+1}.-$), so that father's younger brother is addressed with the elder brother term. Here again is a collapse of generation contrasts: the lower half of the first ascending with the upper half of ego's own. The other extensions of *aNNa* B+ are to cross-collaterals and kinsmen by marriage. In these cases, the contrast between cross- and noncross-categories is neutralized so that elder male cross-cousins and elder sister's husband are addressed in the same way as elder brothers and elder male parallel-cousins.

The term *akka* Z+ is extended in address to FB−Ẇ, MBD+, FZD+, HZ+, FZ−, WM. The use of *akka* Z+ in address to FB−W, MBD+,

FZD+, and HZ+ parallel the extensions of *aNNa* B+ in address. The extension of *akka* Z+ to FB−W rests on the neutralization of the contrast between juniors in parents' generation $(G^{+1}.-)$ and seniors in own generation $(G^{=}.+)$. The extensions to elder female cross-cousins and husband's elder sister rest on the neutralization of the contrast between cross- and noncross-categories. In the extension to father's younger sister both the contrasts between elders in own generation and juniors in parents' generation $(G^{=}.+$ and $G^{+1}.-)$ and the contrast between cross- and noncross-collaterals are neutralized. The extension of *akka* Z+ to WM can be interpreted as an application of the uncle-niece marriage rule (rule 7), by which wife's mother is equivalent to elder sister.

The term *maama* MB is used in address to real and classificatory elder male cross-cousins in addition to those kinsmen who are designated *maava* MB in reference. In address, the term for elder male cross-cousin *baava* drops out entirely and is replaced by *maama* MB. This usage rests on the neutralization of the contrast between the first ascending generation (G^{+1}) and senior kin types in one's own generation $(G^{=}.+)$. On rare occasions the term is extended to cross-cousins younger than the speaker whose names are not known. In these cases the contrast between generations drops out altogether, and *maama* is used to any male cross-kinsman $(K.X.\delta)$.

In address, then, intergenerational equivalence accounts for the common practice of addressing a kinsman with a term which by definition is appropriate to a different generation. This rule accounts for equivalences between the lower half of an ascending generation and the upper half of a descending generation:

muttaata PPF (G^{+3}) → *taata* PF (G^{+2})
taata PF (G^{+2}) → *appa* F (G^{+1})
atte FZ, *cikkappa* FB− $(G^{+1}.-)$ → *akka* Z+, *aNNa* B+ $(G^{=}.+)$
baava PSb$_x$S+ $(G^{=}.+)$ → *maama* MB (G^{+1})

This abundance of neutralizations of generation contrasts is probably a by-product of the preference for intergenerational uncle-niece marriage which results in the collapsing of contrasts of genealogical generation (e.g., where WM is equivalent to Z+, and HM is equivalent to MM, etc.).

In addition, the assimilation of a woman to her husband's family accounts for the extension of *amma* M and *appa* F to a woman's parents-in-law. In these cases the woman is equivalent to her husband: that she calls her husband's parents the same thing he does is a reflection of her absorption into her husband's family. This equivalence is of course very limited, since it applies only to HM and HF in address.

Finally, the extension of elder sibling terms to elder cross-cousins is based on the neutralization of the opposition between X and $\overline{X}$. This may be accounted for by proposing a special alternate of the cross/noncross-neutralization rule (rule 5) for address. This rule was written to operate only in the second or greater ascending and descending generations. By this alternate for address the contrast between cross and noncross may be neutralized for addressees in other generations (e.g., *attige* $PSb_xD+\rightarrow akka$ $Z+$, *maama* $PSb_xS+\rightarrow aNNa$ $B+$). It is also possible, however, to understand these uses of *akka* $Z+$ and *aNNa* $B+$ as similar to metaphoric uses to nonkin (see the next section). However, it seems more likely that these are simply cases of widening based on neutralization of the cross/noncross-opposition. The basis of this neutralization, again, is the preference for uncle-niece marriage which produces equivalences between cross- and noncross-kin such as wife's mother and elder sister, or husband's mother and mother's mother.

Resulting from these extensions, the definitions of the address kin terms are as shown in table 5.2.

The general pattern that emerges from these extensions is a strong preference in address for the unmarked noncross-terms in place of the marked cross-terms.[2] There are several routes for accomplishing this: (1) by the sister's daughter marriage rule, which equates wife's mother (*atte*) with sister (*akka*); (2) by a more general cross/noncross-neutralization rule, which equates elder male or female cross-cousins with elder siblings (FZS = FBS, MBS = MZS); (3) by a wife-assimilation rule, which equates a woman with her husband, so that she addresses his mother in the same way that he does *amma* M. These neutralizations are manifestations of a principle of the system of kin classification discussed in chapter 4: cross-terms are a marked class in contrast to the noncross-terms. Thus when the opposition between cross and noncross is neutralized, it is the unmarked noncross-terms that occur.

It is likely that the preference for noncross terms in address is related to the association of marriage with the cross-category. In Avaruuru marriages are strongly preferred among the closest cross-kinsmen (MBD/FZS, MBS/FZD, MB−/Z+D), who are considered to be *varše*

Table 5.2   **Definitions of Address Kin Terms**

	Root Features					
	Existentially Associated with the Addressee	Kinship	Generation	Relative Age	Linkage	Sex
**taata	A	K	$G^{\geq 2}$			♂
**ajji	A	K	$G^{\geq 2}$			♀
**ammaNNi	A	K	$G^{\geq 2}$			♀
**appa	A	K	1. G^{+1}		L	♂
			2. G^{+2}		L	♂
			3. G^{+1}	+	$//Co^1$	♂
			4. HF			♂
doDDappa	A	K	G^{+1}	+	$\overline{X}$	♂
cikkappa	A	K	G^{+1}	−	$\overline{X}$	♂
ciccappa	A	K	G^{+1}	−	$\overline{X}$	♂
appappa	A	K	G^{+1}	−	$\overline{X}$	♂
**amma	A	K	1. G^{+1}		L	♀
			2. G^{+2}		L	♀
			3. G^{+1}	+	$//Co^1$	♀
			4. HM			♀
doDDamma	A	K	G^{+1}	+	$\overline{X}$	♀
cikkamma	A	K	G^{+1}	−	$\overline{X}$	♀
ciccamma	A	K	G^{+1}	−	$\overline{X}$	♀
cicci	A	K	G^{+1}	−	$\overline{X}$	♀
**aNNa	A	K	G°	+	$\overline{X}$	♂
			G^{+1}	−	$\overline{X}$	♂
**akka	A	K	G°	+	$\overline{X}$	♀
			G^{+1}	−	$\overline{X}$	♀
*maama	A	K	G°	+	X	♂
			G^{+1}		X	♂
atte	A	K	G^{+1}		X	♀
attige	A	K	G°	+	X	♀

*Different from referential definition given in chapter 4.

**Different from referential definition given in chapter 4 and used metaphorically (see next section of this chapter).

Notation (see also appendix 1): A 'existentially associated with addressee'

K 'kinship'
G 'generation'
+ 'elder'; − 'younger'
L 'lineal; $//Co^1$ 'first degree parallel collateral'; X 'cross';
$\overline{X}$ 'non-cross'
♀ 'female'; ♂ 'male'

'preferred relation for marriage' to each other. And when marriages occur between distant relations (*duura sambanda*) or new relations (*hosa sambanda*), the new affinal relatives are terminologically merged into cross-categories. The cross-categories strongly imply marriage ties which are accompanied by increased formality and distance. Many people prefer to avoid these connotations (of affinity, formality, distance) in face to face encounters (e.g., in the speech act) and do so by selecting an address term without the cross-feature.

A second general pattern in the address extensions is that they bring consanguineal and affinal relatives closer generationally: great-grandparents are addressed by grandparent terms, grandparents may be addressed by parent terms, father's elder brother and his wife may be addressed by parent terms, father's younger sister may be addressed by the elder sister term. These relatives are all brought genealogically closer to the speaker by one or one-half of a generation. Similarly, the extension of parent terms to husband's parents, the elder sister term to wife's mother, the elder sibling terms to elder cross-cousins, in addition to neutralizing the cross/noncross opposition, bring the addressee closer to the speaker in terms of genealogical distance, as does the extension of the mother's brother term to elder male cross-cousins.[3]

In summary, the use of kinship terms in address to kinsmen is limited to terms whose definitions include a component of seniority or ascending generation, and it is expected that kinsmen standing in such relationships to the speaker, and thereby entitled to respect, will be addressed with a kinship term. The range of kinship terms for address extends beyond the terms as used to refer to the addressee's relationship to the speaker. These expanded uses which produce alternative designations for many kin types are accounted for by the neutralizations on which they are based. The pattern of neutralizations reveals a preference for avoiding implications of affinity and emphasizing closeness. Thus kin terms in address to kinsmen imply social relationships that are close, but deferential.

Kin Terms in Address to Nonkin

Several of the kinship terms are extended beyond the domain of kinship and used in address to nonkin. The sense of a term when used to nonkin is metaphoric. That is, a term is transferred from the category it literally designates to a fundamentally distinct category. The transfer is based on some similarity between the two categories. The similarity is connoted by the term in its genealogical sense, but becomes part of the definition of the term in its metaphorical sense. Such a transfer establishes a relationship between the two categories by focussing on their similarity (Scheffler and Lounsbury 1971, Bean 1975b).

Establishing definitions of these metaphors is difficult because there is no a priori reason that the results of the transfers in each case will be parallel and will produce a paradigm defined by contrasts on a limited set of dimensions. Therefore, the metaphoric derivations of the terms will be considered independently. A further difficulty in specifying definitions is that metaphor is by nature somewhat vague and ambiguous (Bean 1975b). It is hoped, however, that proposed definitions will accurately portray the way these terms are used metaphorically and present a system that is, as a whole, consistent.

The following terms occur in address to nonkin (each is given with focal kin type and componential definition of the class to which it is applied in reference):

taata	PF	$K.G^{+2}.\male$
ajji	PM	$K.G^{+2}.\female$
ammaNNi	PM	$K.G^{+2}.\female$
tande	F	$K.L.G^{+1}.\male$
taayi	M	$K.L.G^{+1}.\female$
appa	F	$K.L.G^{+1}.\male$
amma[4]	M	$K.\underline{L}.G^{+1}.\female$
aNNa	B+	$K.\overline{X}.\overset{=}{G}.+.\male$
akka	Z+	$K.\overline{X}.\overset{=}{G}.+.\female$

The distinctive characteristic of the corpus is that it contains no terms whose definitions include the feature 'cross'. Only terms defined by the feature 'noncross' are extended to nonkin in address. Terms defined with the feature noncross are the unmarked members of the opposition between cross- and noncross-linkage and stand for both categories when the opposition is neutralized. Moreover, 'cross-linkage' implies the presence or potential of a marriage tie. In the region of Avaruuru all marriages take place within the *jaati*. To address someone of another *jaati* with a kinship term containing the feature 'cross-linkage' would imply the possibility of a marriage tie and would therefore be inappropriate.

All kinship terms signify genealogical relationships between an ego and an alter. Therefore all kinship terms by definition signify a dyadic relationship. Furthermore, genealogical relationships are permanent. The enduring dyadic character of kinship relations renders kinship terms appropriate for address when a speaker wishes to communicate that his relationship to the addressee is more than a momentary one of coparticipation in a speech event (which, for example, is all that is implied by the use of a second-person form). Semantically, the root feature 'kinship' entails a dyadic relationship, and this property of genealogical relationships becomes a feature of the definitions of terms used in address to nonkin as the feature 'dyadic relation' (Dy). Thus, the dyadic relation changes from a genealogical one to a communicative one between a speaker and an addressee.

Earlier it was noted that the only kinship terms occurring in address to nonkin are the senior members of reciprocal sets; and it was observed that the use of these kinship terms in address to kinsmen is an expression of deference. This connotation of deference becomes criterial when kinship terms are used to address nonkin as the indexical component 'polite' **P,** which occurs in the definitions of all kinship terms used for address to nonkin. Because using the kin term in address is an expression of deference for the addressee, the feature 'polite' is indexical; it is existentially associated with what the speaker is *doing* by saying the term.

Other genealogical features (linkage, generation, relative age), of course, drop out when kinship terms are used to address nonkin. The nongenealogical feature 'sex of alter' is retained in addition to the entailed feature 'dyadic relation', the criterial indexical feature 'polite' (previously only an implication), and the root indexical feature 'existentially associated with the addressee'. These features are part of definitions of the metaphoric senses of all of the kinship terms: **A** (existentially associated with the addressee), Dy (dyadic relation), **P** (polite, existentially associated with the act of giving deference), and ♂ (male) or ♀ (female). The distinctions on which the terms contrast are discussed below. The terms will be considered in pairs for male and female designata; the one odd term *ammaNNi* PM will be treated by itself.

1. *taata* PF/*ajji* PM. The term *taata* may be used to address an old man not related to the speaker, but rarely so occurs. The term *ajji* PM may be used to any aged woman (well past child bearing age). In both cases, while the usage is polite, it is not highly deferential. If the speaker wishes to be especially deferential, another term will be chosen, such as *svaami* 'lord' or *ammaNNi* 'great lady'. The two terms *taata* PF and *ajji* PM are distinct from the rest in signifying the age of the addressee. Old age is a property by implication of any category whose

definition includes K.G^{+2}: the feature 'old' (O) is implied by these two features. Thus the definitions of the categories to which *taata* PF and *ajji* PM are applied in metaphoric usage are,

taata **A.Dy.P**.O.♂.
ajji **A.Dy.P**.O.♀.

In the village, any old person not in a position of power (i.e., not the head of a landowning household) may be addressed with these terms regardless of the age, sex, or caste of the speaker.

2. *ammaNNi* PM. The term *ammaNNi* may be used by any speaker to an old woman, but occurs most frequently if the woman is of equal or higher status. It may also be used to women of high social status, especially heads of important households and high status foreigners or outsiders (e.g., doctors) of any age. Although *ajji* PM and *ammaNNi* PM overlap (they have identical foci, PM, and the same class definition, K.G^{+2}.♀, and may be used in address to old women), there is an important distinction between them: *ammaNNi* is considerably more deferential. The difference may be accounted for by the morphological structure of the term. Formally *ammaNNi* PM consists of two parts: *amma* 'mother', metaphorically 'woman, politely', and -*aNNi* an honorific feminine suffix. The term may be glossed 'senior (or great) woman', the seniority ambiguously referring either to age (e.g., 'grandmother', 'old woman') or status (doctor, female head of house).[5] In its use to nonkin, *ammaNNi* PM shares three components with all other metaphoric senses of kin terms: **A.Dy.P**. In addition it has a component 'senior' that may be interpreted either as age or status, and, of course, the component 'female'. Thus, *ammaNNi* **A.Dy.P**.s.♀. In the village, *ammaNNi* is ordinarily used only by A.K. laborers to the female heads of the landowning Kuruba and Tigilru households for whom they work.

3. *tande* F/ *taayi* M. These parent terms do not occur in address to kinsmen. They do, however, occur in deferential address to nonkin, especially in supplication by beggars and A.K.s. The form *taayi* M is used by everyone in address to goddesses. Often these terms occur in combination with the other pair of parent terms as *taayiamma* or *tandeappa* in pleading or as expressions of despair. The term *taayi* may also be used as a polite term of address to any woman, sincerely or ironically. A possible reason for the nonoccurrence of these terms in address to kinsmen and the occurrence in deferential address to nonkin

lies in their etymology. Emeneau (1953) has argued that proto-Dravidian kinship terms occurred with inalienable possessives. Modern Dravidian languages (e.g., Tamil, Gondi, Kui, Kannada) have some kinship terms with *t-* that are unanalyzable, but are explicable as relic forms of a system of inalienable possession. Inalienable possession occurs in some forms in Old Tamil, Kota, Kolami, Gondi, Kui, and Kurukh. The *t-* forms were third-person reflexives, thus, historically, *tande* means 'his/her own father' and *taayi* 'his/her own mother'. I suggest that the analysis of *tande taayi* as etymologically third-person reflexive inalienably possessed kinship terms is relevant for understanding their status as terms for address. The use of third-person forms in deferential address to an individual is a common linguistic phenomenon. Social distance is introduced by treating the addressee as if he were not necessarily present or by symbolically creating a nonintimate triad (speaker+addressee+other). The definitions therefore include a feature 'socially remote' (sr), and the social distance is interpreted as deference (Bean 1970). Thus, as address forms, *tande* F and *taayi* M are socially distant, highly deferential, and therefore inappropriate for address to kinsmen. The metaphoric sense of these terms may be defined:

tande	**A.Dy.P**.sr.♂
taayi	**A.Dy.P**.sr.♀.

4. *amma* M/ *appa* F. This pair of terms for mother and father are the most widely used kinship terms for address to nonkin. These terms are at least occasionally used in polite address to any male or female (except by a man to his wife) in the village. It should be noted that while polite, these are not highly deferential forms. When deference is required in asking for something or addressing someone of much higher status, another term would be selected (e.g., *tande/taayi*). These terms, then, may be defined by those features common to the entire set (**A.Dy.P**) and the dimension of sex of addressee:

appa	**A.Dy.P**.♂
amma	**A.Dy.P**.♀.

5. *aNNa* B+/*akka* Z+. These terms are widely used in address to nonkin who are senior in age or status, but with whom closeness is emphasized. The most plausible explanation of these metaphoric senses is that they are derived from the primary senses of the terms, real siblings (K.Co-L.G⁻.+.♂/♀). Colineals are close, those of the same

sex (brothers or sisters) are, as we have seen, structurally equivalent in the system of kin classification. The status of colineal therefore con-notes closeness. Furthermore, the status of senior sibling connotes so-cial seniority, authority. These connotations of social closeness and seniority become criterial in the metaphoric sense of the terms in ad-dress to nonkin. Thus, in addition to the ubiquitous features **A.Dy.P.**♀/♂, we have 'senior' and 'socially close':

aNNa	**A.Dy.P.**sc.s.♂
akka	**A.Dy.P.**sc.s.♀

In the village these terms are used among members of middle-ranking castes to older (but not aged) addressees, and by members of the low A.K. *jaati* to adult members of higher castes, whether older or younger.

Of the kinship terms used metaphorically in address to nonkin, all but *ammaNNi* 'senior woman', *aNNa* 'senior close man', and *akka* 'senior close woman' may be exchanged by the participants in a speech act. The terms *appa* 'man, politely' and *amma* 'woman, politely' often occur self-reciprocally (e.g., in a conversation between friends); the terms *taata* 'old man', *ajji* 'old woman', *taayi* 'distant woman', *tande* 'distant man' rarely so occur. The significant factor, then, is the feature 'senior', which by definition is asymmetrical. Terms whose definitions include this feature cannot be exchanged.

Table 5.3 gives the kin terms and the definitions of the classes to which they are used metaphorically in address. An indexical component is present in the metaphoric senses of all kinship terms used in address: the root feature of the domain of address, 'existentially associated with

Table 5.3		**Metaphoric Senses of Kin Terms**						
		(1)	(2)	(3)	(4)	(5)	(6)	(7)
			Dyadic				Social	
		Vocative	Relation	Polite	Senior	Old	Distance	Sex
appa	F	A	Dy	P				♂
amma	M	A	Dy	P				♀
taata	PF	A	Dy	P				♂
ajji	PM	A	Dy	P				♀
ammaNNi	PM	A	Dy	P	s			♀
aNNa	B+	A	Dy	P	s		sc	♂
akka	Z+	A	Dy	P	s		sc	♀
tande	F	A	Dy	P			sr	♂
taayi	M	A	Dy	P			sr	♀

the addressee'. This indexical component orients the symbolic and indexical components of the dyadic relationship between addressee and
speaker which may be senior, socially close or distant, and is always
polite (the act of giving deference). The social variables relevant to the
occurrence of these terms in the village are whether or not the addressee
is head of a landowning household (e.g., in the use of *ammaNNi* 'senior
woman'), aged (e.g., *taata* 'old man' and *ajji* 'old woman'), a member
of an untouchable caste (e.g., in the use of *aNNa* 'senior close man', *akka*
'senior close woman' and *ammaNNi* 'senior woman'), and, of course,
the sex of the addressee.

It seems then that Murdock's observations about overlapping terms,
alternative uses, less complete terminologies, and metaphoric designations, quoted in the beginning of this chapter, are all applicable to the
Kannada vocative system. By having analyzed this system we are in a
position to say why. It is that the vocatives signify indexically the
addressee, and the senses of the vocatives, literal, metaphoric, and
connotative, emphasize factors relevant for the face-to-face interaction
in which speaker and addressee are engaged. It is because factors that
relate to the face-to-face sociation of the speech act take precedence in
address that the vocative terminology is usually less appropriate for the
analysis of the system of kin classification itself.

6 | Kannada Personal Names

Personal names are an important part of the Kannada system of address. Incorporating them into the analysis of the address system first requires confronting a problem that has received limited though consistent attention for centuries, and for which an acceptable solution has yet to be found: what do proper names mean? While an interest in proper names can be traced back to the Greeks, the modern concern with their nature seems to have its start with John Stuart Mill. Mill, who treated names in his discussion of the relationship between language and logic, observed that proper names are meaningless labels, in that they tell us nothing of the attributes of the thing named, but serve only to distinguish the named things from each other (Mill 1843). For example, if it is reported that someone saw a *cat* yesterday, it is clear from the meaning of the word *cat* just what sort of a creature was seen: feline, with fur, whiskers, tail, etc. But if it is reported that someone saw *Max* yesterday, it is not possible to be sure just what was seen. *Max* is usually the name of a male human being, but it could also be the name of someone's cat. All that is certain is that yesterday something by the name of *Max* was seen. Thus, Mill argued, a proper name has a reference, stands for something; but it has no sense; it signifies nothing about the characteristics of its denotatum.

Wittgenstein pushed this view to an extreme by

arguing that a genuine proper name had to have a referent in the real world (Wittgenstein 1922), a position which he later abandoned. It is important to make two observations about the extreme position. First, proper names are elements in cultural systems where the existence of a referent in the 'real world' is not an issue; it is the status of the referent in the cultural system that counts (e.g., *Snow White*, *Rama* of the Hindu epic). Second, as Wittgenstein later observed (1953), the status of a linguistic label as a proper name is independent of its having a referent at a particular time. *George Washington* is no less a name because its referent is dead. It is the use, present, past, or potential, of a name as a label for the referent that is crucial.

Gardiner developed Mill's position on the meaninglessness of proper names. As did Mill, he understood that if a name can be interpreted as having a sense (e.g., *Dartmouth* 'the mouth of the Dart'), its meaning is of only secondary relevance and does not affect the label's function as a name, for if the course of the river Dart were to change, the name of the town would remain the same (Mill 1843). For Gardiner, a pure proper name is one that has no sense at all, i.e., conveys no information about the referent. For a name to function as a label, all that is relevant is the association between the distinctive sound of the name and the object it names (Gardiner 1940, p. 43).

Gardiner's association between the distinctive sound of the name and the object it names approaches a clarification of the nature of proper names, a clarification which can be achieved by bringing to it Peirce's trichotomy of signs. The key to understanding proper names is to recognize that they function primarily (though not necessarily exclusively) as indexical signs. That is, names denote their referents not by signifying the attributes of their referents, but by signifying an intrinsic connection to them. In contrast with the case of the person shifters and vocatives discussed in chapters 2, 3, and 5, the intrinsic connection of a proper name and its referent is not to be found in the relation of the name to its situation of utterance, the speech act, but in a culturally posited existential association between the name and its bearer. This culturally 'real' association between name and bearer is often established in a ritual such as christening in which the name is 'bestowed upon' (sometimes by an explicit performative) and after which the name is considered to 'belong to' its bearer.[1] In the case of personal names, which are better studied, the nature of the attachment of the name to its bearer is apparently quite variable (Price and Price 1972, Bamberger 1974, Lévi-Strauss 1966). In

English, for example, 'name' is sometimes synonymous with reputation[2] (e.g., Watergate participant Maurice Stans: "Give me back my good name"), and thus closely associated with the individual. The rules for the use of names will be in part dependent on the quality of the attachment established in a given society.[3]

The defining feature of proper names, then, is one of pragmatic meaning: the intrinsic connection to the bearer. As such the definition carries no information about the bearer except that it is intrinsically connected to the name. Searle has objected to this point of view, agreeing with Mill that proper names have no definite sense (i.e., communicate nothing definite about the attributes of bearers), but not agreeing that consequently they have *no* sense. Searle argues that proper names have senses, but that these are imprecise, a loose set of criteria enabling proper names to fulfill their function: "to refer publicly to objects without being forced ... to come to an agreement as to which descriptive characeristics exactly constitute the identity of an object" (Searle 1969, p. 172). For example, the name *George* conveys the information that the bearer is probably a male human being, though this is not necessarily the case; and the name *Dartmouth* implies that the bearer is probably located at the mouth of the river *Dart,* though this is not necessarily so.

Searle's point that proper names somehow convey some 'imprecise' information about their bearers, is an important one and can be incorporated into this analysis by taking advantage of the concepts of *definition* (*signification*) and *implication* (*connotation*) derived from Morris (1946) and widely used in ethnographic semantics (e.g., Scheffler and Lounsbury 1971). Those attributes of a referent that are necessary and sufficient for it to be denoted by a sign constitute the definition or signification of the sign. The attributes of a referent that are not essential for being denoted by the sign, but that are commonly associated with the sign, are its connotations. For example, it is not necessary (not part of the definition) for an animal to be muddy and disgusting to be called a *pig,* but these are common associations (connotations) of the term. The loose set of criteria that Searle understands as the sense of proper names are nonessential features (connotations or implications) of the meaning of proper names. The definition or essential meaning of proper names is the intrinsic connection to the bearer. The implied attributes of the bearers have two major sources: the classification of names according to the sociocultural categories for which they are appropriate, and the symbolic meaning (in Peirce's sense) of proper names.

While names are fundamentally indexical signs, they may function symbolically as well. It is their indexical signification that makes them proper names, but their symbolic meaning may render them appropriate. For example, *Dartmouth* is appropriate for the name of a town at the mouth of the river Dart, as is *Spot* for a spotted dog. The naming systems of cultures differ in showing preference for names that are symbolically appropriate (for examples see Lévi-Strauss 1966).

Information about the bearer may also be communicated by the classification of names.[4] For example, Americans know that *Champion* and *Trigger* are probably animals, while *Spot* and *Rover,* also animals, are more likely to be dogs. Similarly, we know that *George* is probably a man. However, these classes are not rigid, and this lack of rigidity shows that a name does not in itself signify a class whose members have particular properties, but is merely associated with that class. In English, for example, while *George* is apt to be the name of a man and belongs to the class of names associated with male humans, neither 'male' nor 'human' is part of the definition of *George. George* may be the name of a female (as it is in the Nancy Drew mysteries) or of a dog (as it is of the one belonging to the Richard-Dewars). The result of the classification of names by cultural category is, of course, that when a name is heard (e.g., *George*), there is an expectation that the bearer will have certain attributes (in this case, be a male human being). Thus, while the name (*George*) cannot be said to signify the properties of the cultural category with which it is associated, it can connote that category (*George* does not signify 'male human being', but it does imply 'male human being').[5] Thus, proper names which are defined by a feature of pragmatic meaning, an intrinsic connection to the bearer, can connote attributes of their bearers through the classification of names or through their symbolic meaning (although the latter need not be the case; I can name my white dog *Blackie* if I choose).

It is widely held that proper names function to distinguish individuals (e.g., Bloomfield 1933, p. 205; Jespersen 1922:65). While fundamentally true, this characteristic of proper names requires some clarification. First, if all members of a family are named *Smith,* the name cannot be said to belong to an individual. Here it is easy to see that names do not belong to individuals in the 'real' world, but to units in a cultural system, that is, members of cultural classes. The name *Smith* belongs to a particular family or patriline, a member of the class of families or lines, not to a particular individual. Second, since there are many men named *George*, the name *George* cannot be said to belong to an individual. However, because the defining feature of a proper name is the culturally posited intrinsic connection between the name and its bearer, each of these connections is distinct. Every man named *George* bears his name independently of all other men named *George*.

The distinguishing function of proper names may now be more accurately portrayed. Proper names function indexically to distinguish members of cultural classes, such as persons, families, pets, rivers. In any given social system, to know what things are named is to know those cultural classes whose members are to be distinguished from one another. The naming of people and places is probably universal. The practice of naming members of other classes, e.g., ships or animals, is highly variable.

Because proper names participate in a culturally posited intrinsic connection with their bearers, there must be conventions for establishing such connections. Proper names are bestowed: mountain climbers name mountains; explorers name rivers and lakes; settlers name their villages; people name their children. In a sociocultural system, there are procedures for the selection and bestowal of proper names. For example, among American sects that practice christening, it is the right (and duty) of the parents to select a child's name, but of the priest to bestow the name.

The characteristics of proper names discussed in the preceding pages direct the analysis of Kannada personal names to a consideration of the classes of personal names and the sociocultural categories with which they are associated, the symbolic meanings of personal names and the role of symbolic meaning in the naming system, the selection and bestowal of personal names, and the culturally posited intrinsic connection between personal name and bearer.

Kannada Personal Names

In Kannada only human beings, deities, and places are named. Human beings may have two kinds of names. All people have an *iTTid hesaru* (given or 'put name'), which is usually bestowed in a ceremony after birth pollution has been removed by the first bath (seven or nine days after birth). An astrologer is (or ought to be) consulted in order to ascertain an appropriate name. In Avaruuru all given names are names of gods (*deevar(h)esaru*). In ordinary usage for personal reference or address, the god name is very often accompanied by one of four kinship terms: *amma* literally 'mother', *appa* literally 'father', *akka* literally 'elder sister', *aNNa* literally 'elder brother'. Thus, a man or a woman may be named for the village god, *muneš-vara;* a woman's name form then would be *muniyamma* or perhaps *muniyakka,* and a man's name would be *muniyappa* or *muniyaNNa.* Some people have nicknames (*aDD hesaru*). These usually refer to some personal characteristic, often a physical one (e.g., *guNDappa* 'round man') and frequently an uncomplimentary one (e.g., *kuNTaNNa* 'cripple + elder brother').

The procedure of selecting a name, who selects its, and why, are quite variable. The best way to come to an appreciation of what is involved is to consider some examples. Below are data from four A.K. and three Kuruba families.

Kempamma, an old A.K. woman has six grown children. The oldest, a son, was named *maylaarappa* for their house god (her husband's and hers after marriage). He is usually referred to and addressed by everyone of their caste as *doDDaNNa* 'senior elder brother'. The second child, also a son, was named *biimaNNa* because he was so plump.[6] Bhiima is a name of Shiva of one of the PaaNDava brothers.[7] Kempamma's father went to the astrologer to make sure that the name was an auspicious one. The third child, again a son, was named *doDDmuniyappa* for the village god, Muneshvara, at the instruction of the astrologer. The *doDD –* segment of this name means 'senior' and in fact probably did not become part of the third son's name until after the fourth son was also named for the village god, at the instruction of the astrologer. Because as a child he liked to eat salt, *doDDamuniyappa* is nicknamed *uppnavnu* (from *'uppu'* 'salt' plus *avanu* 'he'). The fourth son is called *cikkamuniyappa* (*cikka* 'junior'). His nickname is *kuN-TaNNa* (from *kuNT* 'lame' and *aNNa* 'elder brother') because one leg is not well formed. The fifth child, a girl, is named *maLamma* for the house god *maylaarappa* and for Kempamma's late elder sister. She is called *muntaayi* (*muni* from the village god and *taayi* 'mother'). Kempamma's mother gave her this nickname. The youngest child, a son, was named *saamaNNa,* for the god Krishna, by Kempamma herself (no horoscope was cast).

MuniyeŋTi, another old A.K. woman, has four sons and a daughter. She reported that the oldest son was named *muniyeŋTa.* The name consists of the name of the village god Muneshvara and the god Venkateshwara, who is both their house god and the god at the popular pilgrimage center Tirupati. MuniyeŋTi said that housegods will protect children named for them. The eldest son is nicknamed *cikkaNNa* 'junior elder brother' because his younger siblings and cousins were too shy to call him by name. Horoscopes cast for the second, third, and fourth sons each revealed the village god, Muneshvara. So the second son is *doD-Damuniyappa* (*doDDa* 'senior'); the third son is *cikkamuniyappa* (*cikka* 'junior'); and the fourth son is *pii muniyappa* (*pii* is the English initial 'P' for the first letter of his father's name). The use of the first letter of the father's name as an initial that is both written in English script and pronounced as a letter of the English alphabet is a recent and very popular innovation. Thus the designations *doDDa* 'senior', *cikka* 'junior', and the English initial *pii* are used to distinguish the three *muniyappa*s. The daughter is named *maarakka* (from the village goddess *maariyamma* and *akka* 'elder sister'). MuniyeŋTi named her for the goddess Maariyamma because she had gone to her temple and pledged that if the goddess would give her a baby girl (after so many sons), the child would be named for her. No horoscope was cast for this child.

DoDDavaLu is the mother of seven children, four of whom have died. Her eldest *piLLigya*, a son, is named for his father's father's father. They had a horoscope cast to make sure that this name was acceptable. The second son, *munpuujiga* is named for the village god, *munešvara*, and the goddess *puujamma*, their house god. When she was sick, DoDDavaLu made a pledge to the house god Puujamma, that if the goddess made her well, the next child would be named for her. The third child, a daughter, *munratna*, was named for the village god Muneshvara, whose name came when the horoscope was cast. They added *ratna* 'precious thing, jewel', an epithet for a god, because they liked it. The fourth child, a girl, was named *muniyeŋTi* for the village god Muneshvara and the god at Tirupati, *yeŋTroonsvaami*. The fifth child, a son, was named *munkišna* for the village god Muneshvara, whose name came in the horoscope, and the the god Krishna because they wanted to. The sixth child, a boy, was named *yeŋTroona* for Venkateshwara, her husband's house god and the god at Tirupati. The last child, a girl, was named *muntaayi* for the god Jademuneshvara, whose temple is in a village not far from Avaruuru. The second part of the name, *taayi* 'mother', they added because they wanted to.

Kariyamma, the youngest of the A.K. women interviewed, has eight children. Her eldest, a girl, was named *puujlakšmi* by her husband's elder sister for the goddesses Puujamma, a deity associated with the A.K. jaati, and Lakshmi the goddess of wealth. She is called *puuji*. An astrologer ascertained that this name was appropriate. The second child and eldest son was named *muniyelliga* for his father's father. The name consists of the names of the village god, Muneshvara and the goddess Yellamma who is special to the A.K. jaati. The third child, a son, was named *muniyeŋTa* for the village god and the god at Tirupati. The fourth child, a girl, was named *timmakka* for her father's father's sister (Timappa is also the name of Vishnu's idol at Tirupati). The fifth child, a daughter, was named *muniyelli* for a pledge that Kariyamma had made to her father's house god (*huTTid mane deevaru* 'house of birth god'), Yellamma. She promised that if the goddess made her well the next child would be named for her. The *muni* segment of her daughter's name is from the name of the village god, *munešvara*. The sixth child, a daughter, was named *maarakka* for the first wife of her (the daughter's) father's brother. The name is derived from the name of the goddess of small pox and the goddess of the village, Maariyamma. Kariyamma's husband named the seventh child, a boy, *naarayNi,* a name of Vishnu. Giving him this name was supposed to prevent them from having more children. The next child, a son, was named *munisvaami* after his father's elder brother who had died. Kariyamma said[8] that they had the astrologer cast a horoscope for each child's name.

NaarayNamma, a young Kuruba woman, is the mother of four children, all girls. The oldest was named *sarsi* for Sarasvati, the Great Tradition goddess of learning, at the suggestion of NaarayNamma's mother. The second, third, and fourth daughters were named *sujaata, sarooja* 'lotus' and *umaa* at the suggestion of her elder sister's daughters. These are currently fashionable names and are unusual in the village. They did not go to the astrologer to have horoscopes cast for any of her children's names, because all of them are girls. The third child is called *piLLi* 'child', 'little one' because her mother's brother preferred the name, and this is the name that stuck.

DoDDaNNa, a Kuruba man, has three children. His eldest, a girl, *reeNuka,* the name of Parashurama's mother, was named by his wife's mother and father, in whose house she was born. The second, also a girl, was named *eemavatti* (from *heema* 'gold' and *vatti* 'a woman possessed of (that) quality'), which, according to doDDaNNa, is the name of a goddess. The names of his daughters were approved by the astrologer after casting their horoscopes. DoDDaNNa's youngest child, a son, was named *raagavendra,* another name for Ramchandra 'moon-like Rama, Rama son of Dasharatha'. The latter name had been given by an astrologer to a son who died. Since *raagvendra* is another name for the same deity (Ramchandra), it was considered proper to bestow the name without going again to the astrologer. The girls' names are unique in the village and are the products of fashion rather than tradition.

Saakamma, a Kuruba woman, has eight children, seven boys and a girl. At the astrologer's instruction their first two boys were named for their deceased father's mother's father, *raamaNNa.* [9] The elder is *raam-candra* and the younger *cikraama* ('junior raama'). The third son is named for Venkateshwara, the god at Tirupati, whose name came in the horoscope. They added *pati* 'king, master' just because they liked it, and the result was the name *yeŋTapati.* The boy is called *pati,* perhaps because Saakamma's husband is *yeŋTappa,* and it is prohibited for a wife to call her husband by name and embarrassing for her to pronounce the name even when it belongs to another. The fourth son is called *raajaNNa* (from *raaja* 'king' and *aNNa* 'elder brother'), but the name that came in the horoscope and was given to him as an infant was *raamamuurti (muurti* 'image'). Once again the astrologer had come up with *raama* in the horoscope. Saakamma reported that she and her family were so tired of the name *raama* that they kept only the first syllable *ra* and made up a different name. They didn't bother going back to the astrologer for the rest of the children. The fifth and sixth sons were named by Saakamma's mother-in-law, who selected the names *jagadiišvara* 'ruler of the world' and *šriinivaasa,* a name of the god Vishnu. The seventh child and only daughter was named *raami* for Saakamma's husband's mother (deceased) at her husband's insistence. The youngest child, a son, was named *sadananda,* a name again selected by Saakamma's mother-in-law. The names selected by Saakamma's mother-in-law were chosen for beauty (*cendakke*). They are all nontraditional names that no adult in the village has and are more closely connected to Great Tradition deities.

The Classification of Personal Names

In the opening section of this chapter, it was suggested that, given the properties of personal names, an analysis of their meaning ought to include the classes of personal names, the symbolic meanings of names, how names are selected and bestowed, and finally, the nature of the connection that is established between the name and its bearer.

There are two labeled classes of names in Avaruuru, the name given at the time of the first ritual bath (*iTTid hesaru*), and nicknames (*aDD hesaru*) acquired later, usually during childhood. All given names are god names (*deevar hesaru*), and every infant receives one. The corpus of such names is enormous, for deities are innumerable, and many have more than one name or epithet by which they are known. Because the gods are classified, the names that people have are classified too. Deities are often associated with particular jaatis, temples, or villages, and therefore their names reveal something of the caste and regional origins of their bearers. Although there is almost an infinite number of names to choose from, the number of individuals in Avaruuru with unique names is small, and a few names are very popular. Most common for the village as a whole are names that contain *yeŋTa* for the widely worshipped god Venkateshwara at the regional pilgrimage center, Tirupati, and *muni* for the village god, Muneshvara. House gods and ancestors are also popular sources of names. Thus a person's name may reveal the region he is from, his jaati, or his family, but this is by no means always the case.

There is another subclassification of god names, not explicitly recognized, that seems to reflect social change. Names of Sanskritic deities, usually chosen by the family rather than the astrologer, are becoming more common in Avaruuru. These names appear to be coming into the village in stages. The Great Tradition names of adults are usually from the epics, the Mahabharata and the Ramayana, from Krishna mythology or from the goddesses of wealth and wisdom, Lakshmi and Sarasvati. The Sanskritic names of children are much more wide ranging, especially among girls: *šaanti* 'peace', *eemavati* 'woman of gold'. One family even reported that a little A.K. girl who had been given a traditional name, *muniyeŋTi* (for the village god and the god at Tirupati), was now called *sarsi* for the Great Tradition goddess of learning, Sarasvati, because she is so fair. (Light skin color is highly desirable, so a little girl with high-class looks ought to have a high-class name.)

A further classification of names is derived from the association of the sex of the god with the name, making some names appropriate only for people of the same sex. Some examples are:[10] *paarvati* only female, name of Shiva's consort; *goovinda* only male, a name of Krishna; *raada* only female, a name of Krishna's beloved; *krišna* only male. However, many names may be used for either males or females: *muni* from the village god, e.g. *muniyamma* (female), *muniyappa* (male); *raama* from the house god Raamdeevaru, e.g. *raamakka* (female), *raamaNNa* (male); *eŋTa* from the god at Tirupati, e.g. *eŋTamma* (female), *eŋTappa* (male). Tentatively, it appears that most local deities may be used for male or female names, but the names of most Sanskritic deities may only be given to humans of the same sex as the deity.

Nicknames (*aDD hesaru*) also fall into implicit classes. The classification is based on their symbolic meaning. Nicknames are always descriptive of their bearers, and are a distinct subclass. A discussion of the classification and meaning of nicknames leads to the consideration of the place of symbolic meaning in personal names.

The Symbolic Meaning of Personal Names

Uncomplimentary nicknames are given primarily to A.K.s, for whom a physical deformity such as deafness, lameness, or scars from a disease may be used as a nickname: *muugi* 'dumb woman', *kuNTa* 'lame man', *gajjiga* 'eczema + male suffix', *sottkayi* 'twisted arm', *kari* 'dark woman', *kaakaa* 'bad fellow'.

Neutral or complimentary nicknames also have appropriate symbolic meaning. Some refer to childhood characteristics (*guNDappa* 'round fellow', *piLLi* 'little one'). Others refer to the bearer's place in the sibling set (*doDDaNNa* 'senior elder brother', *cikkaNNa* 'junior elder brother'). These kinship terms function as names and are used in address and reference where a name ordinarily occurs,[11] unless the bearer is an A.K. In this case speakers of higher jaatis will address and refer to the person as *doDDavanu* 'senior-he' and *cikkavanu* 'junior-he' substituting the third-person pronoun for the kinship term *aNNa* 'elder brother'.

By contrast, all given names (*iTTid hesaru*) are names of deities. Some of these have no symbolic meaning, while others are epithets for deities and refer to some attribute of the deity (e.g. *šaanti* 'peace', *eemavati* 'woman of gold'). In the case of nicknames, the symbolic meaning makes a connection between name and bearer closer, since it is descriptive of an attribute of the bearer, whereas in the case of given names, the symbolic meaning is an attribute of a god.

There are additional formal elements that may be added to given names or nicknames and which have symbolic meaning: *doDDa-* 'elder', *cikka-* 'younger', which distinguish birth order; kinship terms in their metaphoric senses which distinguish social status; and the suffixes *-i* 'female', *-a* or *-ga* 'male', which distinguish the sex of the bearer. Because of the preference for certain sources of names (the village god, the house god) there are often several individuals with the same god name. They are distinguished from each other by the forms *doDDa-* 'elder' and *cikka-* 'younger' (or by an English first initial): *doDDahullurappa, cikkahullurappa*. God names or nicknames often do not occur alone, but have a kinship term suffixed to them. Kinship terms are not part of the name itself, for they are optional; one of several kinship terms may be selected or the kinship term may be omitted. The kinship terms that occur in names are metaphoric signifiers of the status and sex of the named person: *amma* 'woman, politely', *appa* 'man, politely', *akka* 'close senior woman, politely', *aNNa* 'close senior man, politely'. The selection of *amma* rather than *akka*, or *appa* rather than *aNNa*, is a function not only of the attributes of the addressee or referent, but of the relationship of the person denoted to the speaker, so that if a woman's god name is *muni* and she is much younger or of much lower status than the speaker, she will be addressed or referred to as *muni;* if she is of roughly equivalent status or age, she may be addressed and referred to as *muniyamma;* if she is of much higher status but with close social ties, she may be addressed and referred to as *muniyakka*. When names occur without a kinship term, they are likely to end in the common feminine suffix *-i* if the bearer is female (e.g., *raami*), and in the masculine suffix *-a* if the bearer is male (e.g., *raama*). If the god name ordinarily ends in *-i* and the bearer is male, the masculine suffix *-ga* is often added (e.g., *puuji* → *puujiga*).

Selection and Bestowal

The proper procedure for selecting a name is for the father and some close relatives to go to an astrologer shortly after the birth of the baby and before the first ritual bath. The astrologer casts the infant's horoscope and reveals the name or the first syllable of a name appropriate for the child. The practice of going to the astrologer for a name, to the extent to which this procedure is followed, places the astrologer in control of the names bestowed on individuals. It is probably not accidental that almost every name selected for an A.K., in the cases recounted here, was a form of *muni*, for the village god. Nor is it by

chance that many of the names selected for the children of Saakamma
and DoDDaNNa, who are members of the same joint family, were some
variation on *raama*, the name of both the founding ancestor of the
house, RaamaNNa, and the house god, Raamdeevaru. This pattern
recurs in the names of another important Kuruba patriline, many of
whose men are named *hullur-* for their house god, Hullurdeevaru, and
one of their founding ancestors, DoDDhullurappa. It would seem, then,
that the horoscopes cast by the astrologer, who is a Brahmin, most often
come up with the village god as the source of names for the A.K.'s,
emphasizing their ties to the village, and with the names of important
ancestors, especially those named for house gods, as sources of names
for the landowning Kurubas, emphasizing the division of the Kuruba
jaati into patrilines (*vomša*) and patrilineal god groups *deevar vokkaLu*.
It should be noted that names selected by the astrologer for A.K.s and
Kurubas are local (e.g., village gods and house gods). Some of the
fashionable modern names selected by Kurubas and A.K.s for their
children (e.g., *šriinivaasa*) are attached to the Sanskritic tradition.
These are names that Brahmins customarily use and, I suspect a
Brahmin astrologer would be most unlikely to suggest such a name for a
non-Brahmin or untouchable. Thus, names often reflect social status.
To the extent that the Brahmin astrologer has (or did have) control over
selection of names, he controls a significant index of social status.

As was evident in the cases presented, a great many names are given
to children without the benefit of advice from the astrologer. The visit to
the astrologer is neglected most often if the child is a girl or if the child
has several older siblings. In these cases the name is usually selected by
the parents or grandparents of the child, and the child is often named for
a deceased relative, usually on the father's side. In these cases, the
name is frequently selected simply because the parents or grandparents
of the child like it. Names selected for beauty are often those of Sanskritic deities, or are the names of popular movie stars (especially if the
child is a girl). Sometimes the two methods of selection are combined,
so that the relatives of the child add their own choice to that made by the
astrologer. While in most cases the name given to the infant remains
with him for life, in some instances it is replaced, usually during childhood, with one preferred by his relatives (e.g., *umaa* is called *piLLi*,
raamamuurti is called *raajaNNa*).

The name is bestowed in the fifth, seventh, or ninth day after birth.
Until that day, the mother, child, and the members of the household are

aNTu 'polluted'. On that day the mother and child are bathed and brought into the house. The child is placed in its flower-decorated cradle, a basket suspended from the roof beams. At an auspicious time specified by the astrologer, five married women, while swinging the cradle, call the name of the infant five times.[12]

While there are no formalities accompanying the selection and bestowal of nicknames, there is some evidence that Kurubas actively promote the use of uncomplimentary nicknames for the A.K.s (e.g., the name of an A.K. woman, *coudamma,* was changed to *kariyamma* 'dark woman' when she came to Avaruuru as a bride, because the Kurubas thought her very dark). The prevalence among the A.K.s of uncomplimentary nicknames given by the non-Brahmins may be similar to control of Sanskritic names by Brahmin astrologers, a device for manipulating names to reflect rank in the caste system by reserving Sanskritic names for Brahmins and uncomplimentary nicknames for untouchables.

The Relationship of Name and Bearer

In considering the nature of the actual connection between the name and its bearer, the indexicality that is the fundamental property of names, it is necessary to distinguish between god names and nicknames. Every person has a god name that is given to (*iTTid* literally 'placed on') him at the time of the first ritual bath, but the name is not his exclusively; it may belong to several other people in the village simultaneously. More significantly, it does belong to a deity and may also belong to an ancestor. By taking the same name as an ancestor or a deity, one establishes a relationship with that ancestor or deity. The name is doubly indexical, of the man and of the god, and links them. The naming of a child for a god is considered to have an effect on the god as well as on the child. It is considered pleasing for the god (or the ancestor) to have a child named for him. If the name is given for a god who has granted a boon (recovery from an illness; a daughter, rather than a son), the name is given in order to please the god, in repayment for the boon and in hopes of eliciting supernatural protection. Further, if the name came when the child's horoscope was cast, its appropriateness from the point of view of the astrological features of an individual's birth and place in the cosmos is established. Thus, although the name is shared with others as a vehicle for expressing the relationships between the individual and god, and between the individual and the cosmic context of his birth, each connection between the name and the individual who bears it is distinct. Nicknames, by contrast, are derived from something in the social or physical character of the bearer, such as his place in a sibling set (*doDDaNNa* 'senior elder brother'), his habit of talkativeness (*layri yeηTa* 'lawyer yeηTa'), his pockmarked face (*gajjiga,* 'eczema'). In the case of nicknames the actual connection between name and bearer, established by informal agreement expressed in frequent use, is emphasized by the fact that the name refers to an attribute of the individual.

The Meaning and Definition of
Kannada Personal Names

Kannada personal names, like all proper names, signify their actual or potential relationship to a bearer, that is, they are 'existentially associated with the bearer' (represented as the indexical feature **N**). For Kannada, a name is closely connected to the individuality of the bearer astrologically, socially, and, in the case of nicknames, physically. While the given name focuses on the relationship between human beings and deities, the nickname focuses on (by referring to) attributes of its bearer. One of the peculiar characteristics of Kannada personal names is a double indexicality of given names, the association with the bearer on the one side, and the deity on the other, and subsequent beliefs about the relationship between deity and bearer that derive from the one being named for the other.

To say that personal names signify indexically the culturally posited intrinsic connection of name and bearer, and that this is their definition, is not, however, to give an exhaustive account of their meaning. Connotations of personal names arise from the classification of the deities to which the names also belong (and therefore connote region, caste, social status), and from the symbolic signification of nicknames (characteristics of their bearers such as 'dark', 'cripple'). Furthermore, name forms often include segments having symbolic meaning that signify the sex of the bearer, his social status, or his position in a sibling set.

Having established the fundamental indexical signification of personal names, which can be represented formally by the indexical feature 'existential association with bearer' **N**, and having discussed the meaning (both signification and connotation) of Kannada personal names, it is now possible to consider the place of personal names in the semantic structure of the system of address.

7 Personal Names in Address

In address, personal names occur in a variety of forms. The god name or nickname may occur alone (e.g., *puuji, puujiga*) or in combination with kinship terms in their metaphoric senses: *amma* 'woman, politely' (e.g., *puujamma*); *appa* 'man, politely' (e.g., *puujappa*); *akka* 'close senior woman, politely' (e.g., *puujakka*); *aNNa* 'close senior man, politely' (e.g., *puujaNNa*). In addition, the pronominal form *avare,* which is constructed from the third-person plural pronoun *avaru* and the vocative suffix *-e* and metaphorically signifies 'second-person singular, socially remote', may be added to the name forms with *amma* or *appa* (e.g., *puujammanavare* or *puujappanavare*).

God names and nicknames are often used alone to male and female addressees. God name alone is used by almost everyone in the village to address boys of all castes and men of the untouchable caste (A.K.). Name alone is also used among men of touchable castes (Kuruba, Vokkaliiga, BeeDa) who have grown up together, and by older men of touchable castes to younger men whom they have known since boyhood.

Little girls are addressed by god name or nickname alone until they reach puberty, when it is considered appropriate to change to god name with *amma*. Occasionally, however, little girls are addressed by god name with *amma*, usually in the hopes of pleasing them or cajoling them into acting grown-up. After puberty, women who were childhood playmates may continue to address each other by name alone. At puberty or shortly thereafter, a woman moves to her husband's house, usually in another village. There she is addressed by name with a kinship term. In her natal village, however, older people of roughly equal or higher castes may continue to address her by name alone. Adult women of the A.K. caste are often addressed by name alone by higher caste adults and children, although they may also be addressed by god name with *amma*.

Names combined with the kinship terms *amma* 'mother', metaphorically 'woman, politely' and *appa* 'father', metaphorically 'man, politely' are by far the most frequent name forms used in address. (These are also the most common citation forms of names; the usual answer to the inquiry, 'what is your name?')[1] Name with *amma* or *appa* may be used in address to all junior kinsmen (senior kinsmen are usually addressed by a kinship term, but for exceptions see below). In intercaste conversations, the name with *amma* or *appa* is acceptable in address to anyone who is not greatly junior or senior in age or status to the speaker. For example, it would be inappropriate for a Kuruba man to address an A.K. boy by name with *appa*, and it would be rude for an A.K. man to address his landlord by name with *appa*. (He would be more likely to use *svaami* 'lord' in place of a name, or name with *appa* and *avare*). In general, then, name with *amma* or *appa* is very widely used to anyone not greatly different in age or status. There is only one strict prohibition on the use of name with *amma*. A husband always addresses his wife by name alone. It is considered grossly inappropriate to use *amma*. Apparently, the use of a term whose primary meaning is 'mother' to a wife has incestuous overtones (Bean 1975b). A man may, and often does, avoid using his wife's name in address, substituting a pronominal form alone, or if he has to call from any distance, sending a child with his message instead.

God name with the kinship terms *akka* 'elder sister' 'close senior woman' and *aNNa* 'elder brother' 'close senior man' are more restricted in occurrence.[2] The name form with *akka* 'elder sister' may be used by a speaker to an elder kinsman not older than the speaker's parents, such as real or classificatory elder sister (*akka*), elder female cross-cousin (*attige*), father's younger sister (*atte*), or mother's younger sister (*cikkamma*). It may also be used by a speaker to an older woman (who is not aged) of roughly equal or higher caste. In addition, name with *akka* occurs in address to younger women of much higher caste or socioeconomic status.

Name form with *aNNa* 'elder brother' is occasionally used in address to elder kinsmen who are younger than the speaker's parents, such as real or classificatory elder brother (*aNNa*), elder male cross-cousin (*baava* or *maava*), mother's younger brother (*maava*), or father's younger brother (*cikkappa*). Name with *aNNa* is used to members of roughly equal or higher ranking castes who are older than the speaker but not aged. A speaker may use this form to a younger male of considerably higher status[3] (e.g., a poor Muslim widow to a young Kuruba man, or an A.K. woman to a younger Tigilru man).

In general, then, there are occasions on which a speaker will find it appropriate to address nearly everyone in the village with a personal name form (except parents and close kinsmen older than parents). For addressees of about the same or lower age and caste rank, the use of personal name in address will be quite frequent. For persons of greater age or caste rank, the occasions on which the use of a personal name form are appropriate will diminish as the status difference between the speaker and the addressee increases.

Among kinsmen, who are by definition members of the same jaati, there are explicit prohibitions on the use of names in address to one's parents and to one's spouse.[4] It would be considered a serious breach of etiquette to address kinsmen older than parents by a name form. Finally, there are some kinsmen that one may address using a name form, but many people expressed reluctance to do so. For a male speaker, this would include his elder female cross-cousins; and for a female speaker, her younger male cross-cousins. Some women are reluctant to address by name a younger kinsman whose name is the same as her husband's; it is embarrassing to use her husband's name.

The patterns of use of personal name forms in address produce a substantial overlap of name forms that are appropriate for the social identities of a given speaker-addressee dyad. For example, children may be called by god name or nickname alone, or they may be addressed by name with *amma* or *appa;* a person of high status may be addressed by a person of somewhat lower status by name with *amma* or *appa,* and more commonly by name with *aNNa* or *akka* or with *avare* in addition to *amma* or *appa*. The speaker can in this way emphasize some aspect of his relationship to the addressee.

The Definition of Personal Names in Address

There are, then, eight forms of a personal name (n) that occur in address:

n-*i*	female name form ending in -*i*
n-*a* (-*ga*)	male name form ending in -*a* or -*ga*
n + *amma*	name with 'woman, politely'
n + *appa*	name with 'man, politely'
n + *akka*	name with 'close senior female, politely'
n + *aNNa*	name with 'close senior male, politely'
n + *amma(n)avare*	name with *amma* and 'second-person singular, socially remote'
n + *appa(n)avare*	name with *appa* and 'second-person singular, socially remote'

There are no changes in the form of the god name or nickname (n) itself in address, only in the forms that occur with the names.

In chapter 6 it was argued that the defining feature of proper names is the intrinsic connection of name and bearer. All Kannada personal names, then, share this component of pragmatic meaning, which will be written as **N** and glossed 'existentially associated with the bearer'. The significant contrasts among names in address are a function of the meanings of the kinship terms and pronominal forms that occur with names. The name forms contrast along three dimensions: sex of denotatum, social distance, and seniority of status. One of these (sex of denotatum) is an attribute of a person; the other two are attributes of the relationship between persons. The latter are oriented by the indexical component, 'existentially associated with the addressee' **A**, so that 'social distance' and 'seniority of status' apply to the relationship between addressee and speaker. These two relational dimensions are interdependent. Social distance, that is, distance from the private sphere of another, may be interpreted as lack of acquaintance (lack of intimacy) or as deference for a superior (see p. 28). The third dimension, seniority of status, similarly expresses deference for the addressee by acknowledging his superior status.

Sex of denotatum ($\male$ or $\female$) is a symbolic feature of all name forms except those forms consisting of names alone that do not unambiguously refer to a male or female denotatum (see chapter 6). Therefore, the eight name forms that occur in address may be conveniently regarded as four pairs of forms, the members of which are distinguished by the sex of the denotatum (addressee):

Female	Male
n-*i*	n-*a*
n + *amma*	n + *appa*
n + *akka*	n + *aNNa*
n + *ammanavare*	n + *appanavare*

The second dimension, that of social distance, produces three con-trasts: close (sc), remote (sr), and by the neutralization of the opposition between these, neither close nor remote:

Close	Remote	Neither
n-*i*	n + *ammanavare*	n + *amma*
n-*a*	n + *appanavare*	n + *appa*
n + *akka*		
n + *aNNa*		

The feature 'socially close' is signified by name form alone. Evidence that this portion of the definition is correct comes from two sources: the discussion of the nature of names in chapter 6, and the use of name alone in address. A god name or nickname is given to or 'placed' (*iTTid*) on its bearer, that is, an intrinsic association between name and bearer is culturally established. Therefore, the name form alone entails social closeness, since it signifies the addressee by its connection to him. This inference is confirmed by the use of name alone in address to people of roughly the same status, of long acquaintance, frequent asso-ciation, and mutual knowledge, who are therefore intimates, and to addressees considerably junior in age or status. The latter usage is an expression of superiority: the speaker uses a form that signifies the individuality of the addressee, but expects a more distant or deferential form in return.

   Name with *aNNa* 'close senior male, politely' and name with *akka* 'close senior female, politely' also signify 'socially close', which is part of the definition of the metaphoric senses of the kinship terms *aNNa* 'elder brother' and *akka* 'elder sister' (see chapter 5). These name forms are appropriate only to addressees with whom the speaker is acquainted, in contrast to the forms with *avare*, which rarely occur among villagers and much more frequently to high status outsiders. Those superiors with whom the speaker is acquainted and maintains social ties, who are, in other words, socially close, are appropriately addressed by name forms with *aNNa* or *akka*.

By contrast, the definitions of name forms with *avare* include the feature 'socially remote'. The form *avare,* a third-person plural pronoun (*avaru*) with a vocative suffix (*-e*), metaphorically signifies 'second-person singular, distant'. The feature 'socially remote' is produced by the use of a third-person form to denote the addressee, and by the use of a plural form in denoting an individual addressee. Both of these devices introduce distance by transforming the speaker/addressee dyad into a triadic relationship which is inherently more distant (Bean 1970, 1975a). The *avare* name forms are used in the city between casual acquaintances who thereby express respect for each other's privacy. In the village, the name forms with *avare* are used primarily by A.K. laborers to their Kuruba landlords. The feature 'socially remote' may be interpreted as deference for a superior when *avare* forms are not reciprocal, or mutual respect for an equal when *avare* forms are reciprocal. When used nonreciprocally to express deference for a superior, the *avare* forms are apparently more deferential than name forms with *aNNa* or *akka*. The *avare* forms occur almost exclusively in address to the heads of landowning households, the most powerful people in the village.

Name forms with *amma* 'woman, politely' and *appa* 'man, politely' do not signify either 'socially close' or 'socially remote'. Apparently, the metaphoric senses of *amma* and *appa* 'woman/man, politely', when combined with name form alone, result in the neutralization of the contrast between 'socially close' and 'socially remote'. Thus, name form with *amma/appa* is a polite, neither close nor distant, form for address. The fact that names with *amma/appa* are the most widely used name forms in address and are appropriate for everyone except elder kinsmen and those greatly superior or subordinate, suggests that this analysis is correct.

The third and final dimension of contrast that differentiates name forms in address is 'seniority of status'. Only one pair of forms signifies this feature: name forms with *aNNa* 'close senior man' and *akka* 'close senior woman'. The feature signifies the seniority in age or status of the addressee in relation to the speaker. This feature is included in the definitions of metaphoric *akka* and *aNNa*. That it is also distinctive in the definitions of name forms in address that include those kinship terms is evident from the fact that *akka* and *aNNa* are always nonreciprocal in

address (and are the only nonreciprocal name forms).[5] In a speaker/
addressee dyad, the member who receives a name form with *aNNa* or
akka never returns a name form with *akka* or *aNNa*.

All name forms of address are indexical in two ways and are defined
by two common indexical features. As terms of address they are existentially associated with their recipients: 'existentially associated with addressee' **A**. As proper names they signify an intrinsic connection to their
bearers: 'existentially associated with the bearer' **N**. Because name
forms of address include kinship terms or pronouns, they are also symbolic signs which contrast with each other along three semantic dimensions: sex ($\male$ or $\female$), social distance (sc, sr), and seniority (s). Table 7.1
summarizes the definitions of the name forms of address.

Table 7.1   **Componential Definition of Vocative Name-forms**

	Indexical		Symbolic		
	Vocative	Name	Social Distance	Seniority	Sex of Addressee
n-*i*	A	N	sc		$\female$
n-*a*	A	N	sc		$\male$
n-*amma*	A	N			$\female$
n-*appa*	A	N			$\male$
n-*akka*	A	N	sc	s	$\female$
n-*aNNa*	A	N	sc	s	$\male$
n-*ammanavare*	A	N	sr		$\female$
n-*appanavare*	A	N	sr		$\male$

The Socioloinguistic Variables

Analysis of the use of name forms in address yields, on the one hand,
definitions of the name forms of address, and reveals, on the other hand,
aspects of the social identities of the speaker and addressee that are
relevant for judging which form, so defined, is appropriate for a particular addressee, that is, for deciding whether the addressee is to be considered distant from, or senior to, the speaker. The social variables that
most prominently enter into the decision are age, caste rank, and
socioeconomic status. Each of these variables is a continuum that is
divided into segments significant for the selection of name forms.

Two major categories of age appear to be significant for the selection
of name forms in address: child and adult, with a subcategorization of
aged adults. Childhood apparently ends between the onset of puberty at

about 11 or 12 and the age of marriage at 12 to 14 for girls and 15 to 20 for boys. Children of all social groups are treated alike in address. The subcategory of aged adults is significant because old people often continue to use god name or nickname alone to younger adults as they did when the latter were children. The pattern seems to reflect the fact that the residents of Avaruuru are of roughly three generations.[6]

A distinction between untouchable castes and touchable castes is also clearly significant. Moreover, there is a similarity between the use of name forms to children and the use of name forms to untouchables. Both frequently receive name alone not only from those roughly equal in status, but from people of all ages and castes. Both rarely receive the name form with *aNNa* or *akka* (except from junior kinsmen). Children and A.K.s both lack power, and it is this which is expressed in the similar name forms they receive, those marked neither for distance nor for seniority.

Finally, a distinction in socioeconomic status is clear from the villagers' use of the name forms with *avare*. These forms are reserved for the heads of landowning families, male and female, and occasionally for other adults in those households.

The semantic dimensions of social distance and seniority are clearly related to the hierarchies of power and status based on age, caste rank, and socioeconomic status. The three are not independent of each other. Similarities are evident between children and untouchables, and the socioeconomic distinction between landed and nonlanded families is essentially a subdivision of non-Brahmin households. The interrelationship among these variables in the hierarchy of power, caste, and status in the village is expressed in figure 7.1.

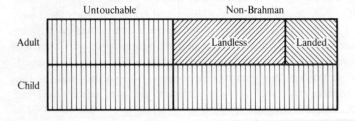

Figure 7.1

8 The System of Address Structure and Function

The Domain

In the first chapter of this monograph, the concept of pragmatic meaning was introduced. It was argued that by admitting pragmatic meaning represented in indexical features it is possible to consider address as a semantic domain, the unity of which is expressed in the shared indexical feature 'existentially associated with the addressee'. The concept of pragmatic meaning is founded on Peirce's theory of signs, which distinguishes three modes of signification: iconic, in which a sign is related to its object by similarity; symbolic, in which a sign is arbitrarily related to its object; and indexical, in which a sign is related to its object through an intrinsic association with it. A sign that is indexical or partly indexical signifies, in its indexical aspect, an existential relationship with its object; that is, it signifies its connection to the nonlinguistic world,[1] to the users and uses of signs, to the social and cultural contexts in which signs occur.

Many ethnologists and linguists have recognized, implicitly, that terms for address constitute a domain-like entity, but without the concept of pragmatic meaning expressed in indexical components, there was no way to show that address constitutes a semantic domain,[2] and terms of address appeared to belong to several distinct domains, such as second-person pronouns, kinship terms, personal names, and titles (e.g., Evans-Pritchard 1948, on names;

Conant 1961, on kinship terms; Brown and Gilman 1960, on pronouns).[3] This kind of division of terms of address is analytically sound.
Its semantic motivation, the relatedness of terms within each subdomain, was discussed in the introduction and provided the basis for the
organization of this book into separate chapters on person shifters,
kinship terms, and personal names. But with the concept of pragmatic
meaning, it is possible to complete the task, combining the analyses of
address terms from each of the subdomains to present the structure of
the system of address as a whole. Once the structure of the address
system is specified, it also becomes possible to disentangle some confusions in other studies of address: to separate the definitions of address
terms from the social variables that are relevant for deciding which term
is appropriate in a given speech event, and to distinguish these from
what address terms *do* in the dyadic sociation of the speech act (that is,
their communicative function).

Additional Address Forms

A few terms of address used by the people of Avaruuru fall outside the
vocabularies of person forms, kinship terms, and personal names. These
are terms that refer to nongenealogical statuses. So few of these occur in
address that they do not warrant a separate chapter. However, they are
of importance because it is these nongenealogical status terms that are
the source of productivity in the system of address. Address terms may
be formed from status terms.

   In Avaruuru, only one form from this class is in frequent use: *svaami*
'master, lord, guru'. In the village, it is used almost exclusively by the
A.K.s to men of landowning families, especially the head of the household for whom the speaker works. It is also used by all village Hindus to
Lingayat and Brahmin priests (none of whom is resident in the village)
and to men who hold very important jobs. On the basis of these uses it
may be tentatively defined: '**A**. high-status. ♂ ', where the status may be
spiritual or temporal. A similarly deferential term that occasionally
occurs in address is formed from *govDa* 'landlord' and the third-person
plural vocative pronoun *avare,* giving the form *goonoore* '**A**. landlord.
socially remote. ♂ '. This form is appropriate only for landlords and is
therefore more restricted in its use than *svaami*. Occasionally the
English borrowing *saar* 'sir' is used to urbanized outsiders like the

Block Development officer or the village health worker. Occasionally also the term *ejamaana* 'master' occurs in address preceded by the vocative particle *ee* 'hey'. The leader of the A.K. community was addressed in this way by Kuruba men: *ee ejamaana*. Similarly, there are a few address forms for children whose names are not known: *ee huDagi* 'hey, little girl'; *mari* 'little one' (although this may also be used as an affectionate nickname).

Theoretically, there is the possibility, though in the village it is rarely exploited, of transforming almost any term that refers to a social status into a term of address. This may be done by preceding it with the vocative particle *ee* as in *ee huDagi* 'hey, little girl' and *ee ejamaana* 'hey master', or by suffixing to the terms the third-person plural vocative pronoun *avare* in order to express deference. For example, *aalu* 'milk' plus *appa* 'man, politely' gives the form *aalappa* 'milkman', which may be combined with the vocative pronoun *avare,* resulting in *aalappanavare* (**A**. socially remote. **P**. milk seller. ♂). These forms are rare in the village. Villagers prefer to use personal names to intimates and subordinates,[4] and kinship terms (in both literal and metaphoric senses) or deferential name forms to addressees senior in age or status.

It is significant that although there are numerous nouns that refer to social statuses and the mechanism for transforming these into vocatives, forms created in this way seldom occur in address and only a few status terms are regularly included in the address system of Avaruuru.

The Structure of the Domain

Address terminology partitions a semantic domain whose root meaning, common to the definitions of all address terms, is the indexical semantic feature 'existentially associated with the addressee'. The semantic structure of the address terminology may be characterized as a loosely articulated paradigm comprised of terms from four subdomains: person, kinship, metaphoric kinship, personal names, plus a few status terms. Each of the subdomains has a root meaning and a number of dimensions on which the meanings of the terms contrast. Some dimensions of contrast occur only in certain subdomains. Other dimensions of contrast are shared by more than one of the subdomains and further serve to unite the whole in a common structure.

Figure 8.1 presents diagrammatically the structure of the domain of address characterized in the preceding paragraph; figure 8.2 gives the details of this structure and provides definitions of each address term. At the top is the root feature 'existentially associated with the addressee' **A**, following which the diagram branches into the several subdomains beginning with the root feature(s) of each of these. The root meaning of the subdomain of second person is the same as the root meaning of the address paradigm (see chapters 2 and 3 for fuller explication). The root meaning of the subdomain of kinship is the symbolic feature 'related by blood and/or marriage' **K**. Kinship terms are also used metaphorically in address. Because their definitions are distinct, having different root features, they are shown in the figure as a separate subdomain. However, the metaphoric senses of kinship terms are derived from the literal senses of kinship terms, and that derivation is represented by an arrow in the figure. The root meaning of the metaphoric kinship terms is the indexical feature 'existentially associated with the act of giving deference' or 'politely' **P**, and the root meaning of the personal name forms used in address is the indexical feature 'existentially associated with the bearer' **N**. Finally, the one or two status terms that occur in the corpus must be fitted into this structure despite the fact that there are too few terms to warrant the inclusion of 'social status' as a separate subdomain.

The Semantic Oppositions and Their Distribution

The definitions of the address terms in each subdomain are distinguished from each other by dimensions of contrast which may be divided into two categories: those which refer to attributes of the addressee and those which refer to attributes of the relationship between addressee and speaker. Dimensions of the former category are number, sex, and age.

The contrast of singular and plural number, realized in the features 'minimal membership' and 'nonminimal membership', is distinctive only in the subdomain of second-person forms. However, it is implicit in the other subdomains, since Kannada nouns are either singular or plural in number. Kinship terms, for example, may take plural suffixes and do so in reference, but not in address. Personal names, on the other hand, which belong to individuals, are not designators of classes and therefore logically cannot be plural. They can and do, however, occur with plural forms (the plural/polite third-person vocative *avare*) in metaphors of deference (see also Bean 1975a). Similarly the status term

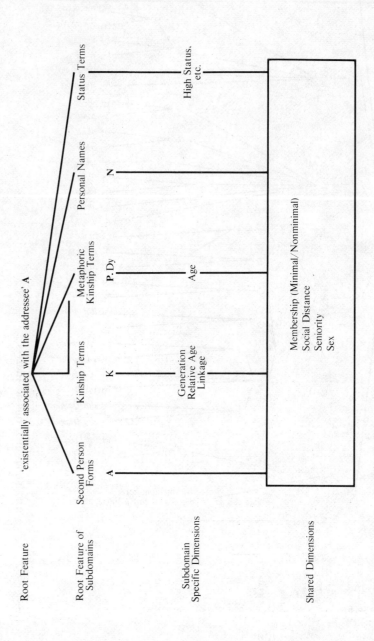

Figure 8.1   The Structure of the Domain of Address

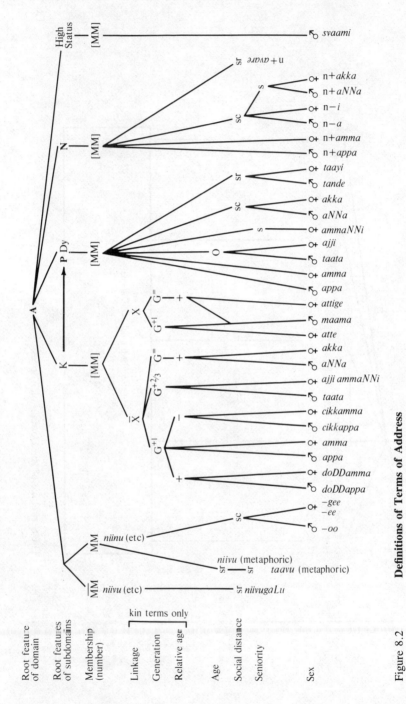

Definitions of Terms of Address

Figure 8.2

svaami may occur in the plural vocative *svaamigaLe*, but when it does, it is for honorific address to an individual. Nearly all address forms in the system denote single addressees. The existence of far fewer terms for plural addressees is a wide-spread feature of address systems (see, for example, Chao 1956, Cooke 1968, Chandrasekhar 1970), and the probable reasons for this phenomenon were pointed out in chapter 1. First of all, plural address terms must be more general in meaning than singular address terms, since they are for use to groups and the composition of a group of addressees may be socially diverse. (Thus, plural person forms, which signify nothing of the social status of the addressees, only their role as addressees, are more appropriate for addressing a group). Secondly, in any case, most speech acts are dyadic, taking place between a speaker and a single addressee.

Age occurs as a dimension of contrast only in the metaphoric senses of kinship terms, where it is realized in the feature 'old' contained in the significata of the grandparent terms: *taata* 'grandfather', 'old man', *ajji* 'grandmother', 'old woman'. Although 'age' is realized nowhere else in the significata of address terms, it is an important social variable for the selection of appropriate address terms. Its role as a sociolinguistic variable is discussed in a later section of this chapter.

Sex of the addressee, realized in the opposition 'male'/'female', is contrastive throughout the corpus of address terms, except in some second-person forms. Kinship terms in their literal senses, their metaphoric senses, and as they occur in name forms, signify the sex of the denotatum. Name forms with no kinship terms are sometimes ambiguous for sex of addressee, although as described in chapter 7, most end in *-i* for female addressees and *-a* or *-ga* for male addressees. Second person singular imperatives can occur with vocative suffixes *-ee* 'female' and *-oo* 'male', or with kinship terms (e.g., *baamma* 'come, woman, politely') that signify the sex of the addressee. The ubiquitousness of features signifying sex of addressee in the address system may possibly be an artifact of the central place of kinship terms whose definitions always include this contrast. However, it is likely that this is more than an accidental characteristic of the address system. Sex and age of addressee are common semantic features and/or relevant sociolinguistic variables in systems of address (see the studies listed on page 107). As in kinship, the probable significance of sex and age in address sytems lies in the fact that these are fundamental aspects of social identity on which qualifications for most ascribed and achieved statuses are contingent (cf. Goodenough 1965a).

Sex, number, and age are the only symbolic dimensions of contrast that are attributes of the addressee. The remainder are attributes of the relationships between addressee and speaker. The relational dimensions are divided into two subclasses: specific and general. The specific relational features are all genealogical and occur in the definitions of kinship terms as they are used in address to kinsmen, and nowhere else in the corpus. The general features are of relations in social space and social hierarchy: social distance and seniority. These features are distinctive in the definitions of person forms, the metaphoric senses of kinship terms, and in personal name forms; that is, in all subdomains except kin classification.

The dimensions of social distance and hierarchy are related. Seniority may be expressed not only by terms which signify seniority, but also by the use of a term which signifies 'socially remote', in the expectation of receiving in return a term which signifies 'socially close' (see the next section). Since there are no terms of address which signify 'junior' (as opposed to 'senior'), the addressee's subordinate status can only be expressed in the speech act by the use of a term which signifies 'socially close'.

Intimacy is expressed in the exchange of socially close terms. Reserve may be expressed in the exchange of socially remote terms, but this usage rarely occurs in the village, though it is common in the city. Intimacy with a status superior may be expressed by a term which signifies both 'socially close' and 'senior'. It is not possible in this system to signify a distant and subordinate addressee, since subordination is expressed only through the feature 'socially close', leaving no way to signify the addressee's social distance.

Social distance and seniority are key dimensions because they are directly related on the one hand to the sociolinguistic variables which influence selection of an address term, and on the other hand to the function of address terms in speech acts. That is, because these are general relational dimensions, the speaker must decide, on the basis of the addressee's social identity, if a 'close', 'distant', or 'senior' term is appropriate. Similarly, because the exchange of 'close' forms expresses intimacy, but a 'close' form exchanged for a 'distant' form expresses hierarchy, the full significance of these forms becomes apparent only when their occurrence in speech acts is considered.

The Place of Kinship Terms in
the Address System

Kinship terms have a special place among the classes of terms that occur in address. They contain the most semantic contrasts; they occur in address to nonkin as well as to kin; they are part of the personal name forms used in address; and they occur with second-person imperatives as vocative suffixes. The dominant place of kinship terms in the Kannada system of address distinguishes it from many others (e.g., American English) and invites consideration of its significance.

Unlike most status terms in the language, which refer to social identities (e.g., *muduka* 'old man', *kuruba* 'member of the Kuruba jaati', *rooTiyappa* 'bread man'), kinship terms refer to social relationships that exist between a propositus and an alter. Kinship terms are therefore eminently suitable for address because they signify a dyadic relationship, and the speech act, similarly, is a dyadic sociation between speaker and addressee. Kinship terms used literally in address signify that the relationship of addressee to speaker is a relationship between two persons in a particular genealogical connection. Kinship terms used metaphorically express a social relationship with the addressee that is similar to one between kinsmen: it is dyadic and implies mutual obligation.

A particular kind of dyadic sociation is implied by the use of a kinship label. In their basic senses, kinship terms refer to genealogical relationships. Genealogical relationships are permanent, a special quality that sets them apart from all other relationships. The implications of this special quality have been discussed by Fortes (1969) as kinship amity, a rule of prescriptive altruism, the special moral obligation that exists between kinsmen in contrast to nonkin; and by Schneider, for American kinship, as "enduring, diffuse, solidarity" (1968, p. 53). Kinship terms in address imply the mutual obligation and closeness that is part of the enduring relationship between kinsmen.[5] In using kinship terms to address kin and nonkin, the people of Avaruuru bring most of those with whom they speak into the realm of prescriptive altruism, if only metaphorically, acknowledging a social relationship that transcends the momentary one of coparticipation in the speech act.

A comparison between city and village usage provides evidence that the use of kinship terms in address implies more durable relationships. City dwellers use far fewer kinship terms to nonkin than do villagers.

People in the village commented on this difference, saying, for example, that *baa taayi* 'come woman (socially remote) politely' (literally 'come, mother') is village language and *bannri* 'come plural/polite' is city language. Similarly, many educated city people drop the kinship terms that usually accompany one's given name (e.g., *mahadeevappa* becomes *mahadeevan*). It may be that relationships among coresidents of a city are more fragmentary, more distant, and more tenuous (that is, without moral obligations) than the relationships among residents of a village like Avaruuru. There, many people are relatives, and those who are not kinsmen are nevertheless in some ways treated similarly, since they participate in intergenerational relationships, with obligations of giving and rights of receiving, and possess the mutual knowledge that arises from long and close acquaintance.

Moreover, genealogical relationships, it is important to recall, are signified by kinship terms in their literal senses and implied by kinship terms in their metaphoric senses. Genealogical relationships, like the attributes of age and sex that are important in the system of address, are primary social identities in which all members of a society participate, and which everywhere are fundamental bases on which other social identities and relationships are built. There is a logic in referring to a universal property of the speech act, the addressee, by terms whose definitions prominently feature those identities, age, sex, and kinship, that are universal building blocks of social systems.

Sociolinguistic Correlates

At this point, a meeting place between semantics and sociolinguistics emerges. The symbolic features in the definition of a term of address are attributes of the person who is addressed or of his relationship to the speaker. Thus, a term whose definition includes the feature 'female' applies by definition to a female denotatum. (Of course, figurative or ironic uses are possible in which the literal definition is opposed to the attributes of a particular denotatum, as when a boy is labeled by a term whose meaning includes the feature 'female' in order to shame him.) Some components of the definitions of address terms apply to specific social identities (e.g., age, sex) or specific relationships (e.g., genealogical). Others are general relational features (e.g., 'dyadic', 'senior', 'socially close', 'socially remote') which do not apply by definition to specific social identities or relationships. It is a sociolinguistic enterprise to discover the correlations between abstract relational components like 'senior' and the relative social identities of addressee and speaker. While this analysis has been almost entirely in semantics, in the course of the analysis the application of address terms to social identities and relationships was described. Where those social identities and relationships are not included as criterial attributes of the definitions, they are the sociolinguistic correlates of the occurrence of the terms. The distinction, I think, is an important one, and has been neglected in many studies of address. For example, Ervin-Tripp (1971, 1972) uses a flow-chart model to represent the important variables in choices among address terms in American English. The discussion is entirely in terms of "sociolinguistic rules," and the sociolinguistic variables are given as "selectors" (e.g., kin, alter higher rank, name known). The outcome of paths through the "flow chart" is a list of possible address forms. Although Ervin-Tripp nowhere says so, the list is ordered from top to bottom by formality or deference, the most formal (title + Last Name) at the top, and the least formal, most intimate, at the bottom (First Name). Thus, for example, "Mrs. + LN" is the outcome of a path including the selectors "alter 15 years older," "married," and "not male" (see Ervin-Tripp 1971, p. 18). But these "selectors" are not, in fact, equivalent: "married" and "not male" are components of the definition of *Mrs.; Mrs.* applies to married women by definition. "Alter 15 years older" is a sociolinguistic variable that influences Ervin-Tripp's choice of "Mrs. + LN" as an appropriate address term.

By contrast Friedrich's analysis of Russian second-person pronouns treats all factors influencing choice equivalently as "cognitive components or discriminations" rather than as sociolinguistic rules (Friedrich 1966, p. 229). The result is that "intimacy" and "the topic of discourse" are similarly "cognitive components." Again, it seems useful to distinguish "intimacy," or closeness, and distance, or "formality," as components of the definitions of the pronouns, while "topic of discourse" is to be understood as a factor influencing the choice of an intimate or formal pronoun. Both Friedrich and Ervin-Tripp confound the significations of terms with the sociolinguistic variables that determine selection among them: Ervin-Tripp makes it all a matter of sociolinguistic rules of choice; and Friedrich, a matter of "cognitive components" (semantic features?). It is analytically necessary to distinguish the defining attributes of the categories from those social and linguistic considerations that lead a speaker to choose a term with a particular definition. In addition to being analytically necessary, this distinction invites consideration of the relationship between definitions and sociolinguistic rules. For example, it seems likely that definitional criteria are more stable than sociolinguistic factors, which influence the choice of a term with a particular definition. Thus we would expect *Mrs.* to apply quite stably to married women, but we might expect more variation over time and space as to whether *Mrs.* is used to addressees of the same age as the speaker, or only of the next ascending generation. The Kannada data have provided some examples of this sort: in Avaruuru the vocative feminine suffix *-ee* is used only by men to their wives, but in villages only fifteen miles away it is also used by fathers to their daughters. Thus, a term whose significata include the feature 'female' applies by definition to female addressees. By contrast, address terms whose significata include general relational features are applied according to the speaker's judgement of the addressee's relative status.

In the discussion of the occurrence of second-person shifters, kinship terms, and personal names in chapters 3, 5, and 7, certain social variables emerged as significant for the choice of an address term whose definition includes general relational features ('close', 'distant', or 'senior'). The relevant social identities paint in broad strokes a picture of village social structure showing some of the major social divisions: one of ritual hierarchy, one of political and economic status, and one of life cycle.

In the use of address terms, members of the untouchable A.K. jaati are often distinguished from those of all other castes. From members of other castes, they receive terms whose definitions include features of social closeness but not terms whose definitions include features of distance and seniority. This special treatment of members of the A.K. caste is an expression of their unique status in the ritual hierarchy of the village. 'A.K.' is an English-style abbreviation (pronounced *yeekee*) for *aadi karnaataka* 'the original inhabitants of Karnataka', a Gandhian name for the caste known as *maadiga,* one of a group of ritually de-filing, untouchable castes. Although untouchability was outlawed in the Indian constitution and this change has been reflected to some extent in the position of A.K.s in Avaruuru, there are still many ways in which the A.K.s are treated specially because of their ritually polluting status. They live in a separate section of the village; members of other castes will not go into their houses (although this shows signs of changing); they are not allowed in the houses of other castes in the village; members of other castes will not take cooked food from them; they are not allowed inside the village temple to worship. This pattern of separating and excluding ritually polluting castes is common throughout South India, where it is often matched at the other extreme of the ritual hierarchy by the Brahmins, who exclude themselves residentially and commensally. Throughout South India the caste hierarchy is commonly segmented into three major portions: Brahmin, non-Brahmin, and untouchable. This division of the caste hierarchy is expressed in the structure of social dialects (Bean 1974b) as well as in the system of address.

A second major social division, one of political and economic status, is expressed in the use of terms of address. This variable is distinct from but interdependent with caste status. The economy of rural India is agricultural. Land is the major form of wealth and is the means of control over people who in the traditional economy exchanged their labor for food. In Avaruuru the dominant caste, owning most of the land and with most of the political power, is the Kuruba ('shepherd') caste. There are, in addition, a few landowners among the Tamil Christian Tigilru caste. In the address system of Avaruuru the regular recipients of deferential address forms (with significata including the features 'senior', 'power holder', and 'socially remote') are those, of whatever caste, who control land and its products: the heads of landowning households, their wives, and, occasionally, their younger brothers. These are the people of political and economic power in the village. They receive deferential forms of address primarily from those who are economically dependent on them. In Avaruuru, a village near a large city, this is a smaller number than in the past, since many now work in or near the city and are no longer dependent on the village economy for their livelihood.

Finally, the use of terms of address regularly expresses the division between adult and child and, among adults, between old people and actively producing and reproducing adults. These are the major divisions of the life cycle in Avaruuru, and three generations copresent in the village. People tend to address members of senior generations with terms whose definitions include the component 'senior' and members of junior generations with terms whose definitions include the component 'socially close'. A few terms (*taata, ajji*) by definition are appropriate only for members of the senior most division.

In summary, the occurrence of general relational features of social distance and seniority correlate with and, therefore, express the ritual division of untouchable and touchable castes; the political and economic division of landless and landed; and the division of the life cycle into child, adult, and old person.

The Function of Address: Arrangements in Social Space

The definition of an address term is inseparable from its occurrence in a speech act, just as its situational use is an inextricable part of its definition. This inseparability of definition and extralinguistic relations is the chief characteristic of pragmatic meaning in which the signification of a sign is an existential relationship with its object (see chapter 1). The character of the extralinguistic relations of address terms requires further consideration: what is it that address terms ''do' in the speech act; what is their communicative function?

All address terms, by definition, are existentially associated with[6] the addressee and, by definition, that is their common function. Given the basic characteristics of the speech act, discussed in chapter 1, the primary and necessary relationship between speech signal and speaker, and the secondary and social relationship of these to the addressee, terms of address function, in effect, to transform speaking into a communicative act, a social phenomenon, by adding the addressee to the naturally prior elements (speaker and speech signal).

While all address terms indicate the addressee, they contrast with each other according to what else, if anything, they indicate or refer to about the addressee or his relationship to the speaker. There are often a number of terms among which the speaker may choose. Occasionally, the address form is obligatory, for example, if a particular grammatical construction is selected that requires the occurrence of a second-person verbal suffix. Sometimes the address form is chosen in order to identify a particular person as the designated recipient of the message. Most often, however, the selection of an address form is not dictated by grammatical constraints or the need for identification, since the context usually makes it clear to whom the message is addressed. Usually, then, the selection is a matter of etiquette. This is how the people of Avaruuru explain the selections they make, and how many analysts of address systems have approached the ordering of their data, either explicitly or implicitly (e.g., Ervin-Tripp 1971, Ullrich 1975, Chao 1956, Brown and Gilman 1960).

The people of Avaruuru explicitly discuss the function of address in terms of etiquette *mariyaade* 'proper conduct, respect, deference' and proper use of language, that is, *bahuvacana* 'polite/plural' or *yeekavacana* 'singular/intimate' (Bean 1975a). Improper use of address terms is spoken of as *garuva maatu* 'prideful, arrogant language'. Occasionally *vidhya* 'rule, manner' or *cenda* 'pleasing' are substituted for *mariyaade,* and *oraTu* 'coarse, overbearing' is substituted for *garuva.* For the people of Avaruuru the function of address is very much a matter of the allocation of deference and the maintenance of proper demeanor.

For example, it is *mariyaade* 'proper conduct' to address one's senior kinsmen with a kinship term, and *garuva* 'arrogant' to address most of them by name. In general it is 'proper conduct' to avoid personal names where other terms, especially kinship terms in their literal or metaphoric senses, may be substituted. Second-person singular forms are 'proper' for almost everyone in the village (except a woman to her husband and A.K. laborers to their landlords). One may, however, give more *mariyaade* 'respect' with second-person plural/polite terms, even though the singular is itself 'proper'. What is considered *mariyaade* 'proper' usage is not only dependent on the definition of the term, but on the context of the speech event in which it occurs. The most important factors are the relative identities of the speaker and the addressee to whom the term is to be applied. What is 'proper' for one's landlord is quite different from what is 'proper' address for one's sister.

What, then, are the connections between etiquette ('proper conduct'), the function of address terms in speech acts, and the semantic structure of the address terminology? I will show in the following paragraphs that this connection is best understood through the concept of social space in the context of the speech act.

It was pointed out in chapter 1 that the speech signal prescribes a face-to-face encounter between a spatially proximate speaker and addressee. The address system functions in the speech act by employing terms expressing hierarchy (seniority, age) and social distance between speaker and addressee, and by the closeness of the relationship between the labeled social identity of the addressee and the individuality of the addressee (Goffman's concept of role distance, 1961). Hierarchy and social distance (especially as 'power' and 'solidarity') are familiar concepts to, and have been used frequently in, the analysis of address. To my knowledge 'role distance' has not been so used (except Bean 1974a) but will be shown below to be of importance. The arrangements in social space, signified or implied by terms of address, adjust the prescribed social form of the speech act to the relative statuses of speaker and addressee in the larger social system by providing for appropriate expressions of deference and intimacy, which the people of Avaruuru discuss as *mariyaade* 'respect, proper conduct'.

The use of space, the arrangements of individuals in space, is apparently an important aspect of all social systems. It seems generally true that proximity to another, being allowed near the other, is a sign of intimacy. Remaining distant, in contrast, is a sign of social distance or subordination. Similarly, the occupation of a large amount of physical space (by size, height, volume) is often a sign of social superiority, power, or high status. In their important paper on second-person pronouns, Brown and Gilman point out that "the dimensions of power and solidarity are fundamental to all social life" (1960, p. 253).[7] People may be related to each other as socially close or distant on the basis of "like-mindedness," mutual knowledge, frequency of interaction, or multiplexity of social relationships; and people may be related to each other by relative power, authority, or status. These two dimensions of social relationships, intimacy and hierarchy, have been shown to be fundamental to social systems, both human and nonhuman (e.g., Tinbergen 1953; Lorenz 1962, on ethology; Goffman 1956; Hall 1959; Sommer 1959, on the analysis of social space; Nadel 1957, on the analytic reduction of role systems to relationships of power and equality).

The identification of hierarchy and intimacy as primitive dimensions of social relationships with an important place in the system of address fits well with the similarly primitive sociobiological dimensions of age, sex, and genealogical connection, on which access to other statuses and roles so frequently depends. The address system is grounded squarely in the primitives of social identities (age, sex, and kinship), and of social relationships (hierarchy and intimacy).

In Avaruuru the social significance of arrangements in space is expressed in ways typically Indian: a woman follows behind her husband when they walk, the houses and wells of the untouchable castes are kept apart from the rest. The significance of spatial arrangements as signs of social relationships is, however, not a simple one. For example, while the higher status, more powerful individuals have control over space, so, in a negative sense, do the untouchables, since they are ritually polluting, and contact with them must be avoided by persons of higher caste status. The social significance of spatial relationships in Avaruuru will not be analyzed here; it is sufficient to point out that arrangements in space have meaning.

More important are linguistic expressions for spatial configurations that are used metaphorically to talk about social relations. It will be noticed that the metaphors are so close to those current in English that it is difficult to give glosses which accurately show the distinction between the literal and metaphoric senses:[8]

	literal sense	metaphoric sense
doDDa/cikka	large, big/little, small	senior, big (important)/ junior
jaasti/kiiLu	more, exceeding/ low, lesser	superior (in status)/ inferior
bahuvacana/ eekavacana	plural/singular	polite, formal, distant/ intimate, informal, derrogatory
heccu/kammi	increase, more/ deficiency, less	superior/inferior

Thus in Avaruuru, spatial expressions of social relations occur in social interaction and in language as well, where words for physical size, number, and amount are used metaphorically to express hierarchy (senior, superior/junior, inferior) and social distance (distant/intimate).

Hierarchy and intimacy are distinct but interrelated. As Goffman (1956) has explained in his discussion of avoidance rituals, deference may be shown by avoiding the private sphere of another. In Brown and Gilman's study, the nonreciprocal exchange of a polite (distant) pronoun for a familiar (close) pronoun is an expression of a power relation. The basis of this expression of power is that the inferior, by giving the polite-distant pronoun, expresses respect or deference through an avoidance ritual; whereas the superior, by returning the familiar-close pronoun, shows that avoidance is not reciprocal, that, as the superior, he is permitted close to the other. In this way social distance may be used to express a hierarchical relationship.

Social distance and hierarchy are signified by address terms with the features 'socially remote' and 'socially close' and 'senior'. Terms that signify 'socially close' may be exchanged to express mutual intimacy; terms that signify 'socially remote' may be exchanged to express mutual distance. Terms that signify 'senior' may be used to acknowledge the addressee's superior status. (Of course, two terms that signify 'senior' cannot be exchanged, since two persons cannot be simultaneously senior to each other.) Finally, the addressee's superior status may also be acknowledged, as was pointed out above, by the use of a term that signifies 'socially remote' in exchange for a term that signifies 'socially close'. Thus, intimacy and hierarchy, as dimensions of the relationship between addressee and speaker, may be expressed in the definitions of address terms or in the combinations of address terms as they are exchanged in speech acts.

The other dimension of social space important to the function of address terms in speech acts is role distance (Goffman 1961), the distance between the addressee as social persona and the addressee as individual. Address terms do not include role distance in their significata; it is implied by what they signify. Role distance in the address system can be usefully approached in Peircian terms as a question of the relationship between sign and object.

Person forms, kinship terms, status terms, and names each signify different aspects of the identity of the addressee. The contrasts can best be expressed as the variation in closeness to or knowledge of the addressee as individual. Second-person forms, as do all terms of address, signify the addressee indexically in his role as coparticipant in the speech act. Some Kannada second-person forms signify only that role, for example, the second-person singular pronoun, *niinu* 'thou'. Other person forms signify in addition social distance ('close' or 'remote') between speaker and addressee (e.g., *niivu* 'thou, polite').

In contrast, kinship terms identify the addressee by signifying indexically the role of addressee, and by signifying symbolically his genealogical relationship to the speaker. When a kinship term is used metaphorically, in address to nonkin, the genealogical components are replaced by components of social distance and seniority. A kinship term used metaphorically, then, identifies the addressee by indicating his role as addressee and referring to general characteristics of his relationship (in terms of hierarchy and intimacy) to the speaker. The status term *svaami* 'lord, master' identifies the addressee, again by indicating his role as addressee, and by referring to his status in the dyadic master-servant role set.

The way in which personal name forms denote their objects is fundamentally different. Kannada names are culturally established indexical signs of individuals. Therefore, when a personal name is used in ad-

dress, it identifies the addressee not only by indicating his role in the
speech act, but by indicating his individuality. Most personal name
forms include a kinship term used metaphorically so that the addressee
is also identified by his relationship to the speaker as 'socially close',
'socially remote', or 'senior'.

By considering how the several classes of address terms identify the
addressee, it is possible to rank the terms according to the distance
between the addressee as social persona and the addressee as individual
and to suggest that terms which identify the most about the individuality
of the addressee are the most intimate. Second-person forms express the
least information about the addressee: only the role of addressee in a
particular and very transient social interaction. Kinship terms in their
literal and metaphoric senses, and the status term *svaami* 'lord, master'
reveal more about the addressee by signifying a social relationship that
transcends the immediacy of the speech act. Personal names, even when
modified by kinship terms, get closest to the addressee as individual
because they denote him by an index of his individuality, his name.

The judgements of the people of Avaruuru concerning what is
mariyaade 'proper conduct, respectful' confirm the conclusion that
hierarchy, social distance, and role distance are of central importance in
the functioning of the address system. Those forms most likely to be
considered *garuva* 'arrogant' rather than 'proper' are personal names
and imperatives with the *-ee* 'socially close female' and *-oo* 'socially
close male' vocative suffixes. These forms function in speech acts to
express close role distance between the individual and his role as addressee, and close social distance between the addressee and the speaker
(although names may be modified with kinship terms and pronominal
forms to lessen the close role distance). Such expressions of intimacy
are appropriate only when the addressee is of junior status or an intimate
of the speaker, otherwise they are likely to be judged 'arrogant'.

Address forms most likely to be considered 'respectful' are those
which signify social distance and seniority (e.g., *taayi* 'socially remote
female', *aNNa* 'socially close senior male') so that the addressee is
referred to as a holder of a social status with respect to the speaker and
not as an individual. Thus, forms which function in the speech act to
express the seniority of the addressee, his social distance from the
speaker, and distance between the addressee as individual and the addressee as participant in the speech act are more often the terms which
are considered 'respectful, proper'.[9]

Respect is shown and proper conduct attended to when the speaker selects a term with the appropriate features of relationship ('socially close', 'socially remote', 'senior') which also allows appropriate distance between the addressee as participant in the speech act and the addressee as individual. That is, any term may be *mariyaade* 'proper, respectful' if the speaker selects it to allow the proper expression of hierarchy, social distance, and role distance.

Terms of address mediate between the social organization of the speech act and the social organization of the larger society to which the participants in the speech act belong. This mediation is accomplished through the adjustment of social space (hierarchy, social distance, and role distance). The prevalence in the literature of descriptions of address terminologies including kinship terms, second-person forms, personal names, and status terms, and their analysis in terms of etiquette, respect, formality, familiarity, and intimacy suggests that the structure and function of the Kannada address system in Avaruuru, while varying in particulars, exhibits basic characteristics of address systems which are everywhere the same.

Appendix 1 | Notation

Indexical Features

S	'existentially associated with the speaker'
A	'existentially associated with the addressee'
P	'existentially associated with the act of giving deference'
A.K.	'existentially associated with speakers of the A.K. jaati'
N	'existentially associated with the bearer' (the defining feature of personal names)

Symbolic Features

A. First occurring in chapters 2 and 3

MM	'minimal membership'
R	'rational'
c	'close'
r	'remote'
sc	'socially close'
sr	'socially remote'
s	'senior'
Dy	'dyadic'
O	'old'
♂	'male'
♀	'female'

B. Primarily in the kin classification system

K	'relation by blood or marriage'
G	'generation' (occurs with superscripts of ± 3 generations, e.g., G^{+2}, and superscript $=$ for own generation, e.g., $G^{=}$)
–	'junior, within generation'

127

	+	'senior, within generation'
	X	'cross-linkage'
	//	'parallel linkage'
	L	'lineal'
	Co	'collateral' (Co¹ 'first-degree collateral, Co² 'second-degree collateral')
	Co-L	'colineal'
Kin type	F	'father'
Notation	M	'mother'
	Z	'sister'
	B	'brother'
	D	'daughter'
	S	'son'
	P	'parent'
	C	'child'
	Sb	'sibling'
	W	'wife'
	H	'husband'
	Sp	'spouse'
Modifiers	−	'younger', follows kintype, e.g., $Z-$ 'younger sister'
	+	'elder', follows kintype, e.g., $B+$ 'elder brother'
	//	'same sex', subscript, e.g., $Sb_{//}$ 'sibling of the same sex'
	x	'opposite sex', subscript, e.g., Sb_x 'sibling of the opposite sex'
	p	'propositus', subscript, e.g., $\male_p$ 'male propositus'
Other	n	'a personal name form'
	$\overline{M}$	'not' overbar, e.g., $\overline{MM}$ 'nonminimal membership'
	−	'minus', precedes notation in some diagrams, e.g., $-MM$ 'minus minimal membership'
	+	'plus', precedes notation in some diagrams, e.g., $+MM$ 'plus minimal membership'

Kin Terms, Foci, and Sample Denotata

Term	Focal Denotatum	Other Denotata	Equivalence Rules
muttaata	PPF great grandfather	FFF MMF FMF MFF FFFB MMFB MFMB FFMB	by definition by definition by definition by definition 3 3 5, 3 5, 3
muttajji	PPM great grandmother	FFM MMM FMM MFM FFFZ MMFZ MFMZ FFMZ	by definition by definition by definition by definition 5,3 5,3 3 3
mumaga	CCS great grandson	DDS SSS SDS DSS ♂BSSS ♂ZSSS ♀ZDDS ♀BDDS	by definition by definition by definition by definition 3 5, 3 3 5, 3
mumagaLu	CCD great grand- daughter	DDD SSD SDD DSD ♂BSSD ♂ZSSD	by definition by definition by definition by definition 3 5, 3

		♀ZDDD	3
		♀BDDD	5, 3
taata	PF	FF	by definition
	grandfather	MF	by definition
		FFB	3
		FMB	5, 3
		MFB	3
		MMB	5, 3
		FMFBS	3, 1, 5, 3
ajji	PM	FM	by definition
ammaNNi	grandmother	MM	by definition
		FFZ	5, 3
		FMZ	3
		MFZ	5, 3
		MMZ	3
		FMFBSW	3, 1, 6, 4, 5, 3
momaga	CS	DS	by definition
	grandson	SS	by definition
		♀BSS	5,3
		♀ZSS	3
		♂BDS	3
		♂ZDS	5, 3
		♂FBSSS	3, 1, 3
		WBS	7, 5, 3
momagaLu	CD	DD	by definition
	granddaughter	SD	by definition
		BSD	3
		ZSD	5, 3
		BDD	5, 3
		ZDD	3
		WBD	7, 5, 3
tande	F		
appa	father		
doDDappa	FB+	FFBS	3, 1
	father's elder	FFFBSS	3, 1, 3, 1
	brother	FMFBDS	3, 1, 3, 1
		FMFBSDH	3, 1, 6
		MZH	3, 2
		HMFBS	3, 1, 6, 1
		(all denotata older than F)	

cikkappa	FB− father's younger brother	MZH MFFBDS	3, 2 3, 1, 4
		HZH ♀ZHZH (all denotata younger than linking P)	6, 7, 4 3, 7, 6, 1
taayi *amma*	M mother		
doDDamma	MZ+ mother's elder sister	FBW FFBSW FMFBSD	3, 1 3, 1, 3, 1 3, 1, 4
		HMZ (all denotata older than linking P)	7, 3
cikkamma	MZ− mother's younger sister	FBW FMBD HFFBD (all denotata younger than linking P)	3, 1 4 3, 1, 6, 1
		HZ ZHZ (denotata older than ego)	7 7, 1
magaLu	D daughter	♀ZD ♂BD ♀HBD ♂FBSD ♀FBDSW	3 3 6, 4, 3 3, 1, 3 3, 1, 6, 1, 3
		♀B−W ♀MMZSSW	7, 3 3, 1, 3, 7, 1, 3
maga	S son	♀ZS ♂BS ♂FBSS ♀HBS ♂MZSS	3 3 3, 1, 3 3, 1 3, 1, 3
aNNa	B+ elder brother	MZS FBS HZH HFFBSDH WZH ZHZH	3, 1 3, 1 6, 6, 1, 3, 1 3, 1, 3, 1, 6, 6, 1, 3, 1 6, 6, 1, 3, 1 6, 1, 6
akka	Z+ elder sister	FBD FFBSD	3, 1 3, 1, 3, 1

		MFBSSW	3, 1, 6, 6
		FFFBSSD	3, 1, 3, 1, 3, 1
		HBW	6, 6
		HFZD	6, 1, 3, 1
		(all denotata older than ego)	
		MBW	7, 3, 1

tamma	B−	FBS	3, 1
	younger brother	MZS	3, 1
		FFBSS	3, 1, 3, 1
		HZ-H	6, 6
		HFZS	6, 1, 3, 1
		HFFBDS	3, 1, 6
		WZH	6, 6
		MFFBDSS	3, 1, 4, 3, 1
		FMFBDSS	3, 1, 3, 1, 3, 1
		(all denotata younger than ego)	
		HZS	7, 3, 1
		HFBSDH	7, 3, 1, 6
		(younger than ego, older than S)	

taŋgi	Z−	FBD	3, 1
	younger sister	MZD	3, 1
		FMFBSDD	3, 1, 4, 3, 1
		MBSW	6
		HBW	6, 6
		WBW	6, 6
		(all denotata younger than ego)	
		HZ+D	7, 3, 1

maava	MB	FZH	6, 4
maama	mother's brother	MFBS	3, 1
		FMFBSS	3, 1, 4
		HF	6
		HFB	3, 6
		MFBSS	3, 1, 7
		FZS, MBS	7
		FMFBSSS	3, 1, 4, 6, 7
		FFBDS	3, 1, 7
		FFFBDSS	3, 1, 4, 7
		ZH	7
		HB	7
		HFFBSS	3, 1, 3, 1, 7
		HMFBSDH	3, 1, 7, 6
		HMFBDS	3, 1, 3, 1, 7
		FFBSDH	3, 1, 3, 1, 7

		FBDH	3, 1, 7
		FMFBSSDH	3, 1, 4, 3, 1, 7
		(these denotata older than ego)	
atte	FZ	FFBD	3, 1
	father's sister	MBW	6, 4
		FMFBSSW	3, 1, 4, 6, 4
		MFBSW	3, 1, 6, 4
		FFFBDSW	3, 1, 4, 6, 4
		WM	6
		WFBW	3, 6, 6, 4
		HM	6
		HFBW	3, 6, 6, 4
aLiya	Sb_xS	♀BS	by definition
	opposite sex sib-	♂ZS	by definition
	ling's son	♀FBSS	3, 1
	(cross-nephew)	♂FBDS	3, 1
		♂FBSDH	3, 1, 3, 6
		DH	6
		DHB	6, 3
		HZS	6, 4
		WBS	6, 4
sose	Sb_xD	♂ZD	by definition
	opposite sex sib-	♀BD	by definition
	ling's daughter	♂BSW	3, 6
	(cross-niece)	DH	6
		WBD	6, 4
		HZD	6, 4
		HFZSD	6, 1, 3, 1
baava	PSb_xS+	FZS	by definition
(not very	elder male	MBS	by definition
common)	cross-cousin	ZH	6
		HB	6
		WB	6
		(denotata older than ego)	
attige	PSb_xD+	FZD	by definition
	elder female	MBD	by definition
	cross-cousin	MFBSD	3, 1
		BW	6
		WZ	6
		HZ	6
		FBSW	3, 1, 6
		HFZSW	6, 1, 3, 1, 6

		♂ Z+D	7, 6
		(all denotata older than ego)	
baamaida	♂ PSb$_x$S−	MBS	by definition
	younger male	FZS	by definition
	cross-cousin	MFBSS	3, 1
	(male proposi-	ZH	6
	tus)	WB	6
		FMFBSSS	3, 1, 4
		(all denotata younger than ego)	
		♂ ZS	7, 6
		FBDS	3, 1, 7, 6
maida	♀ PSb$_x$S−	MBS	by definition
	younger male	FZS	by definition
	cross-cousin	ZH	6
	(female pro-	HB	6
	positus)	HFFBSS	3, 1, 3, 1, 6
		(all denotata younger than ego)	
naadini	PSb$_x$D−	MBD	by definition
	younger female	FZD	by definition
	cross-cousin	HZ	6
		WZ	6
		ZHZ	6, 1
		(all denotata younger than ego)	
		WBD	6, 4, 7, 5
		♂ ZD	7, 6
		♂ MFBSSD	3, 1, 4, 7, 6
		HFBSD	3, 1, 7
		HFFBSSD	3, 1, 3, 1, 7

Notes

Introduction

1. This point is more fully developed in the beginning of chapter 5.
2. They are also known as *maadiga*. During the Gandhian era their caste designation was changed to A.K. (pronounced *yee kee*), and untouchables became known as *Harijans* ("children of god").
3. For analyses of Kannada phonology and grammar see, Bright (1958), Hiremath (1961), Nayak (1967), Ramanujan (1962), Spencer (1950). The best dictionary is Kittle (1894).

Chapter One

1. The term *object* is used with reluctance. To some it means "things" that exist in the "real world." Here it signifies categories (of "things," actions, relationships, etc.) in a sociocultural system. The extracultural status of the object is a separate matter, relevant only when it can be understood as affecting the construction of semiotic systems (see chapter 2).
2. I would like it to be clear that this is my interpretation of the essential distinction between icon, index, and symbol. In this interpretation, indexicality is not a connection between a sign and the "real world" (i.e., extracultural), but between a sign in the linguistic system and an object in the extralinguistic cultural system. Thus the "existential association" is itself a culturally posited (i.e., conventional) association. In this view all signs are conventionally related to their objects: icons are related by a conventionally perceived similarity, indexes by a conventionally perceived existential association, and symbols by convention alone. The problem of indexicality is by no means a simple one. The index is the most interesting and difficult of Peirce's three basic sign-object relations: "Peirce's treatment of the index is not only unfinished . . . but exploratory and so tentative as to

abound in inconsistencies'' (Greenlee 1973, p. 84). ''A study of Peirce's theory of signs is difficult not only because of the unusually fragmentary character of his writings on this subject but also because of the presence of certain inconsistencies and confusions'' (Burks 1949, p. 675). For an analysis of Peirce's sign theory see Greenlee (1973); for a development of Peirce's concept of index see Burks (1949); for Peirce's statements on the subject see ''Logic as Semiotic: The Theory of Signs'' in Buchler (1940), and Peirce's collected writings (1932), especially volume 2.

3. There is much disagreement about the meaning of linguistic signs. Their meaning is variously understood as ideas in the minds of speakers (in the tradition of Locke), verifiable propositions about an extracultural world (e.g., Russell 1940, Frege 1952), the rules for using (or the uses of) linguistic signs (e.g., Wittgenstein 1953). My own view is that linguistic signs stand for cultural categories. The extracultural status of those categories does not constitute meaning, though it may influence the construction of meaning. The cultural categories are apprehended by the users of the sign system but are not reducible to the mental act of apprehension. The task of semantic analysis is to identify the labeled cultural categories (the objects) and to understand how (symbolically, indexically, iconically) and what the signs signify (the definitions) and connote (the implications) about these categories, thus accounting for their senses.

4. In English, for example, there are expressions for different kinds of hearing and hearers. If the receipt of a message is unintentional, we say that it has been *overheard*. If the receipt of the message is intentional, we say that someone was *eavesdropping;* and if modern technology is used, we say that someone has been *bugged*. It would be interesting to compare the ways in which different societies handle this consequence of the public nature of the speech signal.

5. For other approaches to this phenomenon see Jakobson (1960b) and Hymes (1962).

6. The relationship of the receiver to the message and its sender is expressed in the person systems of languages in several ways. In most languages there is a far greater number of terms for addressee than for speaker (Southeast Asia may be an exception). It seems that, because the receiver is not naturally connected to the act of speaking, he must be designated by the speaker, who usually establishes the dyadic association by indicating the addressee in

relation to himself. It is also possible, but much less common, for the speaker to indicate his relationship to the addressee (e.g., mother: 'give Mommy the cup').

Chapter Two   1. Indexical features will be distinguished from symbolic ones by being in bold face type. Appendix 1 is a list of the notations used in the analysis.

2. "A *key* is a multidimensional, and hence often permutable arrangement of attribute oppositions (couplets), which, by their hierarchic application, help to locate (key out) the entities being identified" (Conklin 1964).

3. I have chosen to represent the feature '±minimal membership' as ±MM in order to avoid confusion with the symbol for 'mother' M that occurs in later chapters. See appendix 1.

Chapter Three   1. However, I once heard an older A.K. woman invite a younger Kuruba woman into her house by saying *baaree* 'come + -*ee*'. Both the invitation and its form were highly irregular, since A.K. homes are considered to be too polluting for Kurubas to enter. The speaker in this case was not obviously being rude to her addressee, and I was unable to ask, for fear of embarrassing both of them, the significance of the -*ee* form.

Chapter Four   1. The theoretical and methodological basis for this approach is given in Scheffler and Lounsbury (1971).

2. It is unfortunately impossible to proceed with an analysis of Kannada kinship terminology without saying something about a dispute that has continued to rage over Dravidian kinship systems. The dispute is derived from the fact that a Dravidian kinship terminology appears to divide the universe of relatives into two categories: cross-kinsmen and affines on the one hand, and lineal kinsmen and parallel-collateral kinsmen on the other (though we shall see that this is a clumsy interpretation of the facts). Many students of Dravidian systems, from Rivers onward, have been concerned with this fact. Some have attempted to see this division as a reflection of a binary division of society into a moiety system. Others have noted that many societies having this kind of kinship terminology also practice cross-cousin marriage and have concluded that Dravidian kinship terminology is an expression of a binary division of kinsmen into nonmarriageable and marriageable classes (e.g., Dumont 1953, 1957; Yalman 1969). These views are attractive, because each finds mirrored or expressed in the structure of a terminological system social or cultural facts such as marriage practices or concepts

of affinity and consanguinity. These theories provide an easy route to the discovery of principles simultaneously underlying semantic, social, and cultural systems. The facts are unfortunately far more complex than this variety of theory allows, and it is only by obscuring these facts that the neat structural accounts of Dravidian kinship succeed. Dravidian kinship terminologies do not always coexist with cross-cousin marriage, which in fact in some cases is forbidden (Scheffler 1971). It is not my purpose here to enter into this controversy, but merely to reiterate what Kroeber pointed out many years ago: kin classification systems are linguistic and conceptual phenomena "and can be utilized for sociological inferences only with extreme caution" (Kroeber 1909). Consequently, in order to understand their connection with other social and cultural facts, we must begin with an appreciation of the linguistic facts in their entirety and then proceed to investigate their connections with the social and cultural systems of the people who use them. It is from this point of view that we proceed here, not expecting the kinship terminology to be a map of the rest of the sociocultural system, behavioral or conceptual, but expecting that it will, in discoverable ways, be interconnected with it.

As meaningful linguistic facts, kinship terminologies are fundamentally systems of genealogical classification. They are ego-centered systems of classifying relationships by birth and through marriage (at least there has never been found a kinship terminology that cannot be systematically understood in this way, nor a society without such kinship terminology). This is not to say that kinship *is* genealogy (for to equate kinship with systems of kin classification is an error), nor is it to say that the meanings of kinship terms are *only* genealogical and have no connection with other social and cultural systems. It is to make the modest and limited (and therefore perhaps less interesting) statement that the basic, primary, definitive senses of kinship terms are genealogical and that their connection to kinship systems and to other social and cultural facts is a problem which must be studied in each particular case.

3. The data on which the analysis of Kannada kinship terminology is based was collected from members of the Kannada speaking *jaatis* in Avaruuru (Kuruba, A.K., Vokkaliiga, BeeDa). Most of the data were collected from members of the two most numerous castes: the non-Brahmin middle-ranking Kuruba, and the low-ranking A.K. The forms and their denotata showed no significant

caste variation, and so the data from informants of different castes have been combined in the analysis that follows.

Chapter Five

1. Some special affinal terms are self-reciprocal: *vaargitti* HBW, *biigaru* CSpP.

2. See also Greenberg (1966), in which he argues that in the domain of kinship the following oppositions are universally unmarked to marked: lineal-collateral, elder-younger within generation, consanguineal-affinal.

3. Some individuals also address father as *aNNa* B+ or mother as *akka* Z+. Among some other castes the former usage is common.

4. I know of one case in which *doDDamma* MZ+ was used as a term of address for a nonrelative. The case is special (unlike other nonkin uses of kinship terms) because its use involved a fictive kin tie. The children of a BeeDa man, who was a sharecropper for a Kuruba household, grew up taking their meals in the house of the Kuruba landlord. They learned to address (and still do) the head of that household as *doDDamma,* in recognition, so they reported, of the very special relationship they had with her as children when they were part of the household. She was like an FB+W.

5. This is not the only instance of such ambiguity: *doDDavaru* consists of *doDDa* 'big, senior' and *avaru* 'he, polite'. Once I asked a man who the *doDDavaru* 'senior man' was among the Tigilru jaati, and he inquired whether I meant by age or by landholdings.

Chapter Six

1. It seems to be understood that someone at some time bestowed the name on the person (place, time, or thing). Thus, something has a proper name because it has been *given* it, not because of properties or attributes possessed by that thing. For example, I can't call my cat a *dog,* because he does not have the attributes necessary for belonging to the cultural category 'dog', but I can *name* my cat anything I choose, e.g., *Seymour* or *Popsicle* or even *Dog* (see also Kripke 1972).

2. This is also true of Kannada.

3. It is because the indexical function of names is paramount that proper names are so often not translated or changed (e.g., Chicago, Massachusetts) and remain as some of the few survivors of nearly extinct languages.

4. The classification of names has been given considerable attention by Lévi-Strauss in *The Savage Mind* (1966).

5. Such connotation was no doubt intentional on the part of the author of the Nancy Drew mysteries in naming

a young female character *George,* and it is no doubt taken advantage of by people who name their cats *Seymour* or *Rover.*

6. The connection between the name *biimaNNa* and plumpness is based on the wrestler-like form of Bhiima.

7. The *PaaNDavas* are the heroes of the epic *Mahabharata;* Bhiima is the second son of PaaNDu.

8. But I am skeptical.

9. It is probably significant that their house god is Raamdeevaru.

10. God names are often simplified in ordinary usage. Long names are shortened to two syllables; and initial consonant clusters may be omitted; e.g.:

sumiitra → *suumi*
eemavatti → *eema*
puujalakšmi → *puuji*
candrašeeka → *candra*
krišna → *kisna*
šriinavassa → *siina*

11. Because these nicknames are constructed from kinship terms, they are more deferential than god names and are used more widely in reference and address, that is, where a god name might be inappropriate.

12. Naming customs vary in Karnataka. For example, among Smartha Brahmins five names are bestowed by the mother's brother, who repeats the names five times into the infant's ear. At marriage, the names of women are changed.

Chapter Seven

1. There are a few names whose citation forms contain *akka* 'elder sister'. For example, one always hears *raamakka,* never *raamamma.* Similarly, there are some male names whose citation forms are god name with *aNNa* 'elder brother', such as *raamaNNa* (never *raamappa*).

2. Occasionally the kinship term *aNNa* was added to the god name with *appa* rather than the god name alone (e.g., *maliyappaNNa*). There were not enough occurrences of this form to enable me to make any generalizations about its occurrence.

3. There were some occurrences of this address form that do not conform to these generalizations (e.g., a Kuruba woman to an older A.K. man), but these are exceptional.

4. A woman never addresses her husband by name. Many are reluctant even to speak their husband's name.

5. Two people cannot be senior to each other.

6. Note the similarity, here and in the following para-

graphs, to the situation described for second-person forms in chapter 3.

Chapter Eight
1. This is still a cultural world, not one of some universal 'reality'.

2. Furthermore, it was shown in chapters 2 and 6 that the semantic structure of person shifters and personal names cannot be adequately accounted for unless indexical signification is incorporated into the analysis.

3. The only treatment of an address terminology in its entirety is Chao's paper (1956) on Chinese terms of address, which is a rich and careful description but provides no formal analysis.

4. Such names are usually known, but when they are not, I have heard *maama* MB to a younger male cross-kinsman; *tammayya* B− with an honorific suffix -*ayya* to a younger man whose name was known but was the same as that of the speaker's huband' *ammayya* 'woman + the suffix -*ayya*', and *mari* 'little one' to a child.

5. It should be recalled that in address to kinsmen, kinship terms are manipulated to emphasize the closeness of the relationship between speaker and addressee. See chapter 5.

6. Perhaps more accurately expressed in current parlance: 'laid on' the addressee.

7. Brown and Gilman analyzed the two singular second-person pronouns, one familiar, the other polite, as they are used in many European languages. They posed their analysis in terms of what they called the 'power semantic' and the 'solidarity semantic'. Their analysis is brought into sharper focus and better fit with this analysis if it is pointed out that their term 'semantic' is very loosely used. 'Function' (i.e., 'power function', 'solidarity function') would be more accurate. The definitions of the two pronouns are consistently given as 'second-person singular familiar' and 'second-person singular polite'. These definitions constitute the *semantics,* properly speaking, of the pronouns. What Brown and Gilman analyzed is the occurrence of these pronouns in speech acts, as they are exchanged in speaker-addressee dyads. They found that the exchange of the familiar pronoun functions to express a solidary relationship, the exchange of the polite pronoun functions to express a nonsolidary relationship, and the nonreciprocal exchange of pronouns functions to express a power relationship. Thus two pronouns whose definitions (properly 'semantic') differ in intimacy may occur in speech acts to express solidarity and power, depending on

how the pronouns are exchanged. Expression of solidarity and power are functions, not the definitions, of terms. In this analysis an effort has been made to keep definitions distinct from sociolinguistic factors which influence the selection of a term with a particular definition, and both of these from the function of a term with a particular definition in a speech act.

8. This is, of course, because such expressions in English are similarly used as metaphors for social relationships.

9. Probabalistic statements of what is *mariyaade* 'proper, respectful' have to be used, because only the variables of the identity of the addressee are considered here. In actual fact other variables, such as the intent of the speaker, as well as the more general context, may influence judgments of *mariyaade*.

Bibliography

Aberle, D.F., and Austin, W. M. 1951. A lexical approach to the comparison of two Mongol social systems. *Studies in Linguistics* 9:79–90.

Akmajian A., and Anderson, S. 1970. On the use of fourth person in Navaho, or Navaho made harder. *International Journal of American Linguistics* 36:1–8.

Algeo, John. 1973. *On Defining the Proper Name.* University of Florida Monograph 41.

Alston, William P. 1964. *Philosophy of Language.* Englewood Cliffs, N.J.: Prentice-Hall.

Austerlitz, R. 1959. Semantic components of pronoun systems: Gilyak. *Word* 15:102–9.

Austin, J. L. 1962. *How to Do Things with Words.* New York: Oxford University Press.

Bailey, F. G. 1969. *Stratagems and Spoils.* New York: Schocken Books, Inc.

Bamberger, Joan. 1974. Naming and the transmission of status in a central Brazilian society. *Ethnology* 13, no. 4:363–78.

Bar-Hillel, Y. 1954. Indexical expressions. *Mind,* n.s. 63:359–79.

Barth, Fredrik. 1966. *Models of Social Organization.* Occasional Paper 33. Glasgow: Royal Anthropological Institute of Great Britain and Ireland.

Bates, E., and Benigni, L. 1975. Rules of address in Italy: A sociological survey. *Language in Society* 4:271–88.

Beals, Ralph L. 1961. Kinship terminology and social structure. *Kroeber Anthropological Society Papers* 25:129–48.

Bean, Susan S. 1970. Two's company, three's a crowd. *American Anthropologist* 72:562–64.

————. 1972. Kannada kinship terminology: Use and meaning. Ph.D. dissertation. Columbia University.

————. 1974a. An exploration into the semantics of social space in Kannada. In *Structural Approaches to South India Studies,* edited by Harry Buck and Glen Yocum. Chambersburg, Pa.: Wilson College for the Liberal Arts.

————. 1974b. Linguistic variation and the caste system in South Asia. *Indian Linguistics* 35:277–93.

————. 1975a. The meanings of grammatical number in Kannada. *Anthropological Linguistics* 17:33–41.

————. 1975b. Referential and indexical meanings of *amma* in Kannada: Mother, woman, goddess, pox, and help! *Journal of Anthropological Research* 31:313–30.

Beck, Brenda E. F. 1972. *Peasant Society in Konku.* Vancouver: University of British Columbia Press.

Becker, A. L., and Oka, I. Gusti Ngurah. 1973. Person in Kawi: Exploration of an elementary semantic dimension. Ms.

Befu, Harumi, and Norbeck, E. 1958. Japanese usages of terms of relationship. *Southwestern Journal of Anthropology* 14:66–86.

Beidelman, Thomas O. 1963. Terms of address as clues to social relationships. In *Modern Sociology: An Introduction to the Study of Human Interaction,* edited by A. W. Gouldner and H. P. Gouldner. New York: Harcourt, Brace and World.

Benveniste, E. 1956. La Nature des pronoms. In *For Roman Jakobson,* edited by M. Halle et al. The Hague: Mouton.

Berlin, B. 1963. A possible paradigmatic structure for Tzeltal pronominals. *Anthropological Linguistics* 5, no. 2:1–5.

Berreman, Gerald D. 1972. Social categories and social interaction. *American Anthropologist* 74:567–86.

Bloomfield, Leonard. 1933. *Language*. New York: Holt, Rinehart, and Winston.

Bogardus, E. S. 1933. A social distance scale. *Sociology and Social Research* 17:265–71.

———. 1959. *Social Distance*. Yellow Springs, Ohio: Antioch Press.

Bright, William. 1958. *An Outline of Colloquial Kannada*. Indian Linguistics Monograph Series 1, Poona.

Brown, Roger, and Ford, M. 1961. Address in American English. *Journal de la Société des Américanistes de Paris* 62:375–85.

Brown, R., and Gilman, A. 1960. The pronouns of power and solidarity. In *Style in Language*, edited by T. A. Sebeok. New York: John Wiley and Sons.

Buchler, I. R., and Freeze, R. 1966. The distinctive features of pronominal systems. *Anthropological Linguistics* 8, no. 8:78–105.

Buchler, Justus, ed. 1940. *The Philosophy of Peirce: Selected Writings*. New York: Harcourt, Brace and Co.

Bühler, L. 1934. *Sprachtheorie*. Jena.

Burks, A. W. 1949. Icon, index, and symbol. *Philosophy and Phenomenological Research* 9:673–89.

———. 1951. A Theory of Proper Names. *Philosophical Studies*, vol. 2.

Capell, A. 1966. *Studies in Sociolinguistics*. The Hague: Mouton.

Carpenter, C. R. 1958. Territoriality: A review of concepts and problems. In *Behavior and Evolution*, edited by A. Roe and G. G. Simpson, pp. 229–50. New Haven: Yale University Press.

Chandrasekhar, A. 1970. Personal pronouns and pronominal forms in Malayalam. *Anthropological Linguistics* 12:246–55.

Chao, Yuen Ren. 1956. Chinese terms of address. *Language* 32:217–41.

Chomsky, Noam. 1957. *Syntactic Structures*. The Hague: Mouton.

―――. 1965. *Aspects of the Theory of Syntax*. Cambridge, Mass.: MIT Press.

Codrington, R. H. 1885. *Melanesian Languages*. Oxford: Clarendon Press.

Collinson, William Edward. 1961. *Indication: A Study of Demonstratives, Articles, and Other 'Indicators'*. Baltimore: Waverly Press.

Conant, Francis P. 1961. Jarawa kin systems of reference and address. *Anthropological Linguistics* 3:20–33.

Conklin, Harold C. 1962. Lexicographical treatment of folk taxonomies. In *Problems in Lexicography*, edited by F. W. Householder and S. Saporta. Bloomington: Indiana University Research Center in Anthropology, Folklore, and Linguistics.

―――. 1964. Ethnogenealogical method. In *Explorations in Cultural Anthropology*, edited by W. H. Goodenough. New York: McGraw-Hill.

Cooke, Joseph R. 1968. *Pronominal Reference in Thai, Burmese, and Vietnamese*. University of California Publications in Linguistics 52. Berkeley: University of California Press.

Das, Sisir Kumar. 1968. Forms of address and terms of reference in Bengali. *Anthropological Linguistics* 10, no. 4: 19–31.

Delorme, E., and Dougherty, R. C. 1972. Appositive NP constructions: We, the men; we men; I, a man; etc. *Foundations of Language* 8:2–29.

Dorian, Nancy C. A substitute name system in the Scottish Highlands. *American Anthropologist* 72:303–19.

Dumont, L. 1953. The Dravidian kinship terminology as an expression of marriage. *Man* 54:34–39.

―――. 1957. *Hierarchy and Marriage Alliance in South Indian Kinship*. Occasional Papers of the Royal Anthropological Institute, no. 12. London.

Eder, James F. 1975. Naming practices and the definition of affines among the Batak of the Philippines. *Ethnology* 14:59–70.

Edmonson, Munro S. 1958. *Status Terminology and*

the *Social Structure of North American Indians*. American Ethnological Society Monograph 30. Seattle: University of Washington Press.

Emeneau, M. B. 1938. Personal names of the Todas. *American Anthropologist* 40:205–23.

———. 1941. Language and social forms: A study of Toda kinship terms and dual descent. In *Language, Culture, and Personality*, edited by L. Spier, A. I. Hallowell, and S. S. Newman. Menasha, Wisc.: Banta.

———. 1950. Language and non-linguistic patterns. *Language* 26:199–209.

———. 1953. The Dravidian kinship terms. *Language* 29:339–53.

———. 1974. Ritual structure and language structure of the Todas. *Transactions of the American Philosophical Society*, n.s., vol. 64, no. 6.

Ervin-Tripp, Susan M. 1971. Sociolinguistics. In *Advances in the Sociology of Language II*, edited by J. Fishman. The Hague: Mouton.

———. 1972. On sociolinguistic rules: Alternation and co-occurrence. In *Directions in Sociolinguistics*, edited by J. J. Gumperz and D. Hymes. New York: Holt, Rinehart, and Winston.

Evans-Pritchard, E. E. 1948. Nuer modes of address. *The Uganda Journal* 12:166–71.

Fillmore, Charles J. 1966. Deictic categories in the semantics of come. *Foundations of Language* 2:219–27.

———. 1968. The case for case. In *Universals in Linguistic Theory*, edited by E. Bach and R. Harms. New York: Holt, Rinehart, and Winston.

———. 1970. Subjects, speakers and roles. *Working Papers in Linguistics, Ohio State University Computer Information Science Research Center* 4:31–63.

———. 1971a. *Santa Cruz Lectures on Deixis*. Bloomington: Indiana University Linguistics Club.

———. 1971b. Verbs of judging: An exercise in semantic description. In *Studies in Linguistic Semantics*, edited by C. J. Fillmore and D. T.

Langendoen. New York: Holt, Rinehart, and Winston.

Fischer, J. L. 1964. Words for self and others in some Japanese families. *American Anthropologist* 66, no. 6, pt. 2: 115–26.

Forchheimer, Paul. 1953. *The Category of Person in Language.* Berlin: W. de Gruyter.

Fortes, Meyer. 1969. *Kinship and the Social Order.* Chicago: Aldine.

Foster, G. M. 1964. Speech forms and the perception of social distance in a Spanish speaking Mexican village. *Southwestern Journal of Anthropology* 20:107–22.

Foster, Michael. 1974. When words become deeds. In *Explorations in the Ethnography of Speaking,* edited by R. Bauman and J. Sherzer. London: Cambridge University Press.

Freedman, D.; Cannady, C.; and Robinson, J. 1971. Speech and psychic structure: A reconsideration of their relation. *Journal of the American Psychoanalytic Association* 19:765–79.

Frege, Gottlob. 1952. On sense and reference. In *Philosophical Writings,* edited by P. Geach and M. Black. Oxford: Oxford University Press.

Frei, Henri. 1944. Systèmes de déictiques. *Acta Linguistica* 4:111–29.

Friedrich, Paul. 1966. Structural implications of Russian pronominal usage. In *Sociolinguistics,* edited by William Bright. The Hague: Mouton.

Gai, G. S. 1940. The inclusive and exclusive first person plural in Kannada. *Bulletin of the Deccan College Research Institute,* pp. 411–12. Poona.

Gale, Richard M. 1964. Is it now now? *Mind* 73:97–105.

————. 1967. Indexical signs, egocentric particulars, and token reflexive words. *The Encyclopedia of Philosophy* 4:151–55. New York: Macmillan.

Gardiner, A. H. 1940. *The Theory of Proper Names.* London: Oxford University Press.

Garfinkel, H., and Sacks, H. 1969. On formal structures of practical actions. In *Theoretical Sociology: Perspectives and Developments,* edited by J. C. McKinney and E. Tiryakian. New York: Appleton-Century-Crofts.

Garvin, Paul L., and Riesenberg, S. 1952. Respect behavior on Ponape: An ethnolinguistic study. *American Anthropologist* 54:201–20.

Geertz, Clifford. 1973. *The Interpretation of Cultures.* New York: Basic Books.

Geoghegan, William. 1971. Information processing systems in culture. In *Explorations in Mathematical Anthropology,* edited by Paul Kay. Cambridge, Mass.: MIT Press.

George, K. M. 1962. The personal termination in the Dravidian verb with special reference to Malayalam. *Indian Linguistics* 23:39–48.

Goffman, Erving. 1955. On face-work. *Psychiatry* 18, no. 3: 214–31.

———. 1956. The nature of deference and demeanor. *American Anthropologist* 58:473–502.

———. 1961. Role distance. In *Encounters,* edited by E. Goffman. New York: Bobbs-Merrill.

Goodenough, W. H. 1956. Componential analysis and the study of meaning. *Language* 32:195–216.

———. 1965a. Personal names and modes of address in two Oceanic societies. In *Context and Meaning in Cultural Anthropology,* edited by M. E. Spiro, pp. 265–76. New York: Free Press.

———. 1965b. Yankee kinship terminology: A problem in componential analysis. *American Anthropologist* 67, no. 5, pt. 2: 259–87.

———. 1965c. Rethinking status and role. In *The Relevance of Models for Social Anthropology,* ASA Monograph 1, edited by Michael Banton. New York: Praeger.

———. 1967. Componential analysis. *Science* 156:1203–9.

Greenberg, Joseph. 1966. Language universals. In *Current Trends in Linguistics,* vol. 3, edited by T. Sebeok. The Hague: Mouton.

Greenlee, Douglas. 1973. *Peirce's Concept of Sign.* The Hague: Mouton.

Gregor, Thomas. 1974. Exposure and seclusion: A study of institutionalized isolation among the

Mehinacu Indians of Brazil. *Ethnology* 13, no. 4: 333–50.

Hall, Edward. 1959. *The Silent Language.* New York: Doubleday.

Halliday, M. A. K. 1970. Functional diversity in language as seen from a consideration of mood or modality in English. *Foundations of Language* 6:322–61.

Haugen, E. 1975. Pronominal address in Icelandic. *Language in Society* 4:323–39.

Hearn, G. 1957. Leadership and the spatial factor in small groups. *Journal of Abnormal Social Psychology* 54:269–72.

Hiremath, R. C. 1961. *The Structure of Kannada.* Dharwar: Karnatak University.

Hockett, Charles D. 1960. The origin of speech. *Scientific American,* September 3–10.

Hockett, Charles F. 1963. The problem of universals in language. In *Universals of Language,* edited by J. H. Greenberg. Cambridge, Mass.: MIT Press.

Householder, Fred W. 1955. Review of *The Category of Person in Language,* by Paul Forchheimer. *Language* 31:93–99.

Hymes, Dell. 1955. Review of *The Category of Person in Language,* by Paul Forchheimer. *International Journal of American Linguistics* 21:294–300.

————. 1962. The ethnography of speaking. In *Anthropology and Human Behavior,* edited by T. Gladwin and W. C. Sturtevant. Washington, D. C.: Anthropological Society of Washington.

————. 1971. Sociolinguistics and the ethnography of speaking. In Association of Social Anthropologists, Monograph 10, *Social Anthropology and Language,* edited by Edwin Ardener. London: Tavistock.

————. 1972. On personal pronouns: 'Fourth' person and phonesthematic aspects. In *Studies in Linguistics in Honor of George L. Trager,* edited by M. Estellie Smith. The Hague: Mouton.

Ingram, David. 1971a. Typology and universals of

personal pronouns. In *Working Papers on Language Universals* 5, Language Universals Project. Stanford: Committee on Linguistics.

———. 1971b. Toward a theory of deixis. *Papers in Linguistics* 4:37–54.

Jacobsen, William H. 1967. Switch-reference in Hokan-Coahuiltecan. In *Studies in Southwestern Ethnolinguistics,* edited by Dell Hymes and William Bittle, pp. 238–63. The Hague: Mouton.

Jain, Dhanesh Kumar. 1969. Verbalization of respect in Hindi. *Anthropological Linguistics* 11, no. 3:1, 79–97.

Jakobson, R. 1939. Signe zéro. In *Mélange Bally.* Geneva.

———. 1957. *Shifters, Verbal Categories, and the Russian Verb.* Cambridge: Russian Language Project, Department of Slavic Languages and Literatures, Harvard University.

———. 1960a. Comments on Brown and Gilman. In *Style in Language,* edited by T. A. Sebeok. New York: John Wiley and Sons.

———. 1960b. Concluding statement: Linguistics and poetics. In *Style in Language,* edited by T. A. Sebeok. New York: John Wiley and Sons.

———, and Halle, M. 1956. *Fundamentals of Language.* The Hague: Mouton.

Jespersen, Otto. 1964 [1922]. *Language: Its Nature, Development, and Origin.* New York: W. W. Norton.

Jones, O. F. 1965. The pronouns of address in present-day Icelandic. *Scandinavian Studies* 37:245–58.

Jonz, Jon G. 1975. Situated address in the United States Marine Corps. *Anthropological Linguistics* 17, no. 2:68–77.

Karunatilake, W. S. 1975. Pronouns of address in Tamil and Sinhalese: A sociolinguistic study. *International Journal of Dravidian Linguistics* 4:1.83–96.

Karve, Irawati. 1968. *Kinship Organization in India.* Bombay: Asia Publishing House.

Kittel, Rev. F. 1894. *A Kannada-English Dictio-*

nary. Mangalore: Basel Mission Book and Tract Depository.

Kripke, Saul. 1972. Naming and necessity. In *Semantics of Natural Language*, edited by D. Davidson and G. Harman. New York: Humanities Press.

Kroeber, A. L. 1909. Classificatory systems of relationship. *Journal of the Royal Anthropological Institute* 39:77–84.

Kuno, Susumo. 1972. Pronominalization, Reflexivization, and Direct Discourse. *Linguistic Inquiry* 3:161–96.

Lakoff, Robin T. 1970. Tense and its relation to participants. *Language* 46:838–50.

———. 1971. If's, and's, and but's about conjunction. In *Studies in Linguistic Semantics*, edited by C. J. Fillmore and D. T. Langendoen. New York: Holt, Rinehart, and Winston.

Lambert, W. E. 1967. The use of tu and vous as forms of address in French Canada: A pilot study. *Journal of Verbal Learning and Verbal Behavior* 6:614–17.

Langacker, R. 1969. Pronominalization and the Chain of Command. In *Modern English Studies*, edited by D. Reibel and S. Schane. Englewood Cliffs, N.J.: Prentice-Hall.

Lévi-Strauss, Claude. 1966. *The Savage Mind*. Chicago: University of Chicago Press.

Little, K. B. 1965. Personal space. *Journal of Experimental Social Psychology* 1:237–47.

Locke, John. 1706. *An Essay Concerning Human Understanding*. London.

Lorenz, Konrad. 1962. *Behavioral Aspects of Ecology*. Englewood Cliffs, N.J.: Prentice-Hall.

Lounsbury, F. G. 1956. Semantic analysis of the Pawnee kinship usage. *Language* 32:158–94.

———. 1964. The structural analysis of kinship semantics. In *Proceedings of the Ninth International Congress of Linguists*, edited by H. G. Hunt, 1073–93. The Hague: Mouton.

Loving, Richard. 1973. Awa kinship terminology and its use. *Ethnology* 12:429–37.

Lyons, John. 1968. *Introduction to Theoretical Linguistics*. Cambridge: Cambridge University Press.

McCawley, J. D. 1968. The role of semantics in grammar. In *Universals in Linguistic Theory*, edited by E. Bach and R. T. Harms. New York: Holt, Rinehart, and Winston.

————. 1971. Tense and time reference in English. In *Studies in Linguistic Semantics*, edited by C. J. Fillmore and D. T. Langendoen. New York: Holt, Rinehart, and Winston.

McIntire, Marina L. 1972. Terms of address in an academic setting. *Anthropological Linguistics* 14:286–91.

McKaughan, H. 1959. Semantic components of pronoun systems. *Word* 15:101–2.

Malinowski, Bronislaw. 1965 [1935]. *Coral Gardens and Their Magic*. Vol. 2, *The Language of Magic and Gardening*. Bloomington: Indiana University Press.

Martin, S. E. 1964. Speech levels in Japan and Korea. In *Language in Culture and Society*, edited by D. Hymes. New York: Harper and Row.

Mbaga, K., and Whiteley, W. H. 1961. Formality and informality in Yao speech. *Africa* 31:135–46.

Metzger, D., and Williams, G. 1967. Patterns of primary personal reference in a Tzeltal community. *Estudios de Cultura Maya*, vol. 6.

Middleton, J. 1961. The social significance of Lugbara personal names. *The Uganda Journal* 25:34–42.

Mill, John Stuart. 1843. *System of logic*. London.

Milner, G. B. 1961. The Samoan vocabulary of respect. *Journal of the Royal Anthropological Institute* 91:296–317.

Moles, Jerry A. 1974. Decisions and variability: The usage of address terms, pronouns, and languages by Quechua-Spanish bilinguals in Peru. *Anthropological Linguistics* 16:442–63.

Morris, Charles W. 1938. *Foundations of the Theory of Signs*. International Encyclopedia of

Unified Science 1, no. 2. Chicago: University of Chicago Press.

———. 1946. *Signs, Language and Behavior.* New York: Prentice-Hall.

Murdock, G. P. 1949. *Social Structure.* New York: Macmillan.

Nadel, S. F. 1957. *The Theory of Social Structure.* Glencoe, Ill.: Free Press.

Nayak, H. M. 1967. *Kannada: Literary and Colloquial.* Mysore: Rao and Raghavan.

Needham, R. 1965. Death names and social solidarity in Penan society. *Bijdragen tot de Taal-, Land- en Volkenkunde* 121:58–76.

Opler, Morris E. 1937. Apache data concerning the relation of kinship terminology to social classification. *American Anthropologist* 39:201–12.

Peirce, Charles S. 1932. *The Collected Papers of Charles Sanders Peirce.* Vol. 2, *Elements of Logic,* edited by Charles Harshorne and Paul Weiss. Cambridge: Harvard University Press.

———. 1940. Logic as Semiotic: The Theory of Signs. In *The Philosophy of Peirce,* edited by J. Buchler. New York: Harcourt, Brace.

Pittman, Richard S. 1948. Nahuatl honorifics. *International Journal of American Linguistics* 14:236–9.

Postal, P. M. 1970. On so-called pronouns in English. In *Readings in English Transformational Grammar,* edited by R. A. Jacobs and P. S. Rosenbaum. Waltham, Mass.: Ginn.

Price, Richard, and Price, Sally. 1972. Saramaka onomastics: An Afro-American naming system. *Ethnology* 11, no. 4: 341–67.

Ramanujan, A. K. Ms. 1962. A generative grammar of Kannada. Ph.D. Dissertation, Indiana University.

Ross, J. R. 1970. On declarative sentences. In *Readings in English Transformational Grammar,* edited by R. A. Jacobs and P. S. Rosenbaum. Waltham, Mass.: Ginn.

Roys, R. L. 1940. Personal names of the Mayas of

Yucatan. *Carnegie Institution Contributions to American Anthropology and History* vol. 6, no. 31.

Russell, B. 1940. *An Inquiry into Meaning and Truth.* New York: W. W. Norton.

Sadock, Jerrold M. 1974. *Toward a Linguistic Theory of Speech Acts.* New York: Academic Press.

Sankaran, C. R. 1939. Reconstruction of the proto-Dravidian pronouns. *Bulletin of the Deccan College Research Institute* 1:96–105.

Scheffler, Harold W. 1971. Dravidian-Iroquois: The Melanesian evidence. In *Anthropology in Oceania,* edited by L. R. Hiatt and C. Jayawardena. Sydney: Angus Robertson.

———. 1972. Kinship semantics. *Annual Review of Anthropology* 1:309–28.

———. 1976. The 'meaning' of kinship in American culture: Another view. In *Meaning in Anthropology,* edited by K. Basso and H. Selby. Albuquerque: University of New Mexico Press.

———, and Lounsbury, Floyd G. 1971. *A Study in Structural Semantics: The Siriono Kinship System.* Englewood Cliffs, N.J.: Prentice-Hall.

Schneider, David M. 1968. *American Kinship: A Cultural Account.* Englewood Cliffs, N.J.: Prentice-Hall.

———. 1969. Componential analysis: A state of the art review. Ms.

———. 1970. What should be included in a vocabulary of kinship terms. Ethnology Science Council of Japan, *Eighth Congress of Anthropological and Ethnological Sciences,* vol. 2. Tokyo.

———, and Homans, G. C. 1955. Kinship terminology and the American kinship system. *American Anthropologist* 57:1194–208.

Schreiber, Peter A. 1972. Style disjuncts and the performative analysis. *Linguistic Inquiry* 3:321–47.

Searle, John R. 1969. *Speech Acts.* Cambridge: Cambridge University Press.

Sebring, James M. 1969. Caste indicators and caste

identification of strangers. *Human Organization* 28:199–207.

Shanmugam Pillai, M. 1972. Address terms and the social hierarchy of the Tamils. In *Proceedings of the First All-India Conference of Dravidian Linguists, 1971,* edited by V. I. Subramoniam, pp. 424–32. Trivandrium: Dravidian Linguistic Association of India.

Silverstein, Michael. 1973. Linguistics and anthropology. In *Linguistics and Neighboring Disciplines,* edited by R. Bartsch and T. Vennemann. North Holland Linguistics Series, no. 4.

————. 1976. Shifters, linguistic categories and cultural description. In *Meaning in Anthropology,* edited by K. H. Basso and H. A. Selby. Albuquerque: University of New Mexico Press.

Simmel, Georg. 1902. The number of members as determining the sociological form of the group. *American Journal of Sociology* 8, no. 1: 1–46, 158–96.

————. 1950. *The Sociology of Georg Simmel.* Translated by Kurt H. Wolf. Glencoe, Ill: The Free Press.

Sinha, G. S., and Sinha, R. C. 1967. Exploration in caste stereotypes. *Social Forces* 46:42–47.

Sjoberg, Andrée F. 1968. Telegu personal names: A structural analysis. *Studies in Indian Linguistics,* edited by Bh. Krishnamurthi. Poona: Deccan College.

Slobin, Dan I. 1963. Some aspects of the use of pronouns of address in Yiddish. *Word* 19:293–202.

————; Miller, S. H.; and Porter, L. W. 1968. Forms of address and social relations in a business organization. *Journal of Personality and Social Psychology* 8:289–93.

Sommer, Robert. 1959. Studies in personal space. *Sociometry* 22, no. 3:247–60.

————. 1962. The distance for comfortable conversation. *Sociometry* 25, no. 1: 111–16.

————. 1969. *Personal Space:* Englewood Cliffs, N.J.: Prentice-Hall.

Southworth, Franklin C. 1974. Linguistic masks for

power: Some relationships between semantic and social change. *Anthropological Linguistics* 16, no. 5:177–91.

Spencer, Harold. 1950. *A Kanarese Grammar*. Revised by W. Perston. Mysore: Wesley Press.

Staal, J. F. 1970. Performatives and token-reflexives. *Linguistic Inquiry* 1:373–81.

Steinzor, B. 1950. The spatial factor in face-to-face discussion groups. *Journal of Abnormal Social Psychology* 45:552–55.

Subbaiya, K. V. 1919. *The Pronouns and Pronominal Terminations of the First Person in Dravidian*. Madras: Madras Government Press.

Subrahamanayam, P. S. 1967–68. Personal pronouns in Dravidian. *Bulletin of the Deccan College Research Institute* 28:202–17.

Tambiah, S. J. 1968. The magical power of words. *Man* 3, no. 2, 175–208.

———. 1973. Form and meaning of magical acts: A point of view. In *Modes of Thought,* edited by R. Horton and R. Finnegan. London: Faber and Faber.

Thomas, D. 1955. Three analyses of the Ilocano pronoun system. *Word* 11:204–8.

Thomson, D. F. 1946. Names and naming in the Wik Monkan tribes. *Journal of the Royal Anthropological Institute* 6:157–68.

Tinbergen, N. 1953. *Social Behavior in Animals*. London: Methuen.

Trager, George L. 1943. The kinship and status terms of the Tiwa languages. *American Anthropologist* 45:557–71.

Tyler, Stephen A. 1969. Context and variation in Koya kinship terminology. In *Cognitive Anthropology,* edited by Tyler. New York: Holt, Rinehart, and Winston.

Ullrich, Helen E. 1975. Etiquette among women in Karnataka: Forms of address in the village and the family. *Social Action* 25:234–48.

Vatuk, Sylvia. 1969a. Reference, address, and fictive kinship in urban North India. *Ethnology* 8, no. 3: 255–72.

Waldron, R. A. 1967. *Sense and Sense Develop-*

ment. The Language Library. Kent, Eng.: Tond-
bridge Printers.

Watson, Michael O. 1974. Proxemics. In *Current
Trends in Linguistics,* edited by T. Sebeok, 12:
311–44. The Hague: Mouton.

Weinreich, Uriel. 1963. On the semantic structure
of language. In *Universals of Language,* edited by
J. Greenberg, pp. 123–27. Cambridge, Mass.:
MIT Press.

Wells, Rulon. 1968. Distinctively human semiotic.
Social Science Information 6, no. 6: 103–24.

Wittgenstein, Ludwig. 1953. *Philosophical Investi-
gations*. Translated by G. E. M. Anscombe. Oxford: Oxford University Press.

———. 1961 [1922]. *Tractatus Logicophiloso-
phicus*. Translated by D. F. Pears and B. F.
McGuiness. London: Routledge and Kegan Paul.

Wonderly, William. 1952. Semantic components in
Kechua person morphemes. *Language* 28, no. 3:
366–76.

Yalman, Nur. 1969. The semantics of kinship in
South India and Ceylon. In *Current Trends in
Linguistics,* edited by T. Sebeok, 5:607–26.

Zwicky, Arnold M. 1974. Hey, what's your name.
In *10th Regional Meeting of the Chicago Linguistic Society,* pp. 787–801. Chicago: Chicago Linguistic Society.

Index